KLING STUBBINS

KLING STUBBINS

PALIMPSEST

images
Publishing

Published in Australia in 2008 by
The Images Publishing Group Pty Ltd
ABN 89 059 734 431
6 Bastow Place, Mulgrave, Victoria 3170, Australia
Tel: +61 3 9561 5544 Fax: +61 3 9561 4860
books@imagespublishing.com
www.imagespublishing.com

National Library of Australia Cataloguing-in-Publication entry:

Title: KlingStubbins: palimpsest.

ISBN: 978 1 86470 295 8 (hbk.)

Subjects: KlingStubbins (Firm)
                Architectural firms – United States.
                Engineering firms – United States.
                Architecture.
                Commercial buildings.

Dewey Number: 720.973

Coordinating editor: Robyn Beaver

Art direction and design: Jason Trojanowski

Production by The Graphic Image Studio Pty Ltd, Mulgrave, Australia
www.tgis.com.au

Pre-publishing services by Splitting Image Colour Studio Pty Ltd, Australia
Printed by Everbest Printing Co. Ltd. in Hong Kong/China

IMAGES has included on its website a page for special notices in relation to this and our other publications. Please visit www.imagespublishing.com.

TABLE OF CONTENTS

EVOLUTION

EFFECT

KlingStubbins

Palimpsest

PALIMPSEST

BRADFORD WHITE FISKE, FAIA

It is not possible to create buildings for the future unless they are predicated on cognizance of the past. History is elemental, an irreducible constituent of the entity of architecture. We perceive the materiality of architecture modified by the issue of orientation and factored by physical distance; but we also understand its presence in terms of absence—that which was, remains influential. Our ghosts, while ephemeral, are real.

There will never be a blank slate. Super-impositions of a vague image of what once was lie coincident with not always concrete manifestations of changes to come. We are ever evolving, changing into a different and more complex firm with different and more complex issues to address. Our work is unconstrained by a strict architectural vocabulary; ungoverned by a single guiding principle—except a desire to realize architecture of distinction.

We acknowledge that architecture is unable to exist as an independent act. All who come upon great architecture are met first, not by shelter or solidity, proportion or magnitude, but by the highest ambitions of the client and the enduring will of the architect to serve them. Architecture is a profoundly optimistic wager that our aspirations today will be inspiring tomorrow; that our enduring expressions will reach toward others.

While our design studios are highly collaborative—fueled by the vitality of our architects and engineers—the truly vital pairing is that of our clients' ambitions with the will and talent of the architect to fulfill them. Fostering those ambitions is our goal, with the confidence that the architect's vision will serve them well.

Stewardship of a design vision is a journey that must advance deliberately, with conviction and focus, while remaining highly critical and aware. Along this path, constraint and promise are oftentimes paradoxically embraced as opportunities, traveling forward with purposeful determination while keeping the most open mind. This balance of pragmatism and inspiration is the essence of design.

Societal and cultural conditions inspire and shape our architecture. Expectations of propriety, often particular to either place or time, connote parameters within which one is to define design. We have always needed to be aware of the present character of urban conditions; the habits and mores of those who presently dwell cannot be ignored, but equally importantly, they are the basis upon which we conjecture as to the city's future. Society and culture are advanced by architecture, and, in turn, architecture by them.

The immediacy of the natural and man-made context simultaneously defines and expands the province of architecture. Climatic and historical data act to establish specificity of response, while the fleeting sensations realized from blowing wind, shifting vistas, memories, and connotations, all defy dogmatic measure. Patterns of movement, solar orientation, the density of adjacent development are all factors as significant as the design program. Once built, the program, thought to be contained within the building, leaps across those imagined boundaries—it is no longer novel but insinuated within the context. We find promise in the unscripted life of a building.

Singular as a fingerprint, the physical character of the site, whether limited or beautiful, must be sympathetically addressed by a design premise that amplifies its promise and acknowledges its constraints. Contending with the fundamental nature of a place is not only our duty, but also a primary source of our inspiration. Vestiges of what had been remain either visible or discoverable in our best work.

Architecture, as we endeavor every day for it to be understood, must endure—its true contribution is meaningless if the design is not built soundly. Masterpieces of design accrue cultural meaning slowly, often long after their initial purpose and context have metamorphosed, thus their longevity is crucial. Across many diverse regions and idioms of design, these masterpieces share a common trait: the highest technique of building. Advanced building technology expresses a belief that we are pursuing meaningful, enduring art. From the painstaking care of master draftsman, to the guild secrets of masons, truly significant buildings were at once bound to tradition and obliged to innovate. While our available technologies have evolved, we must remain committed to advance our techniques. Within this tradition, architecture and engineering were never intended to be separate. Their seamless integration has produced the vast majority of our landmarks—it was a modern approach then as now.

Our architecture has always been confronted with the task of assisting the human race to establish control over the environment, but there is the equally attendant issue of preserving the environment concurrent with its willful adaptation. Our designs attempt to reconcile the many contradictory demands placed upon them without the sacrifice of artistry for expediency, or more importantly, without impingement on the immediate surroundings. We understand the world that we inhabit as ripe with implication and potential, and we endeavor to do no harm as we pursue the production of both structure and meaning.

We see our firm today, we see ourselves, as the effect of our history, our work, our aspirations—like our approach to design—an initial vision consistently challenged and enhanced as it is brought to reality. Within our work, dualities are consciously plentiful: the perception of mass is conjoined with weightlessness; materiality is offset by transparency; function is enriched by experience; and technology is coupled with whim. We aspire for an architecture of evanescence, not truly transitory, but highly mutable as the play of light shifts perception from surface to void, from the immediate to the reflected, from the present to the future. We endeavor to realize design not primarily about forms and surfaces, but identifiable by the forces that act upon it.

We, as architects, embrace architecture as process; a process that aspires to realize a sophisticated symbiosis of the character of context and the culture of the client, while striving to reach the level of symbolic discourse articulated by culture as a whole. We explore because the investigation of possibilities offers the intimation of something not entirely known—prefigurations of the unrealized, reiterations of the forgotten, the prospect of poetic transformation. We identify with the writings of Proust and his focus on involuntary memory, the evocation of recollections without conscious effort; and with the work of Robbe-Grillet, the fractured timelines and plots that suggest different meanings to different people. We admire the paintings of deChirico, inspired by the bright sunlight, and, reciprocally, the deep shadow of the Mediterranean, rich with association while fraught with enigma; and the mystery and incongruity produced by Delvaux.

Neither our practice, nor our work, can be fully understood as a simple narrative; for architecture never conveys a singular story. Instead it should be viewed as a palimpsest, with our memories influencing our dreams.

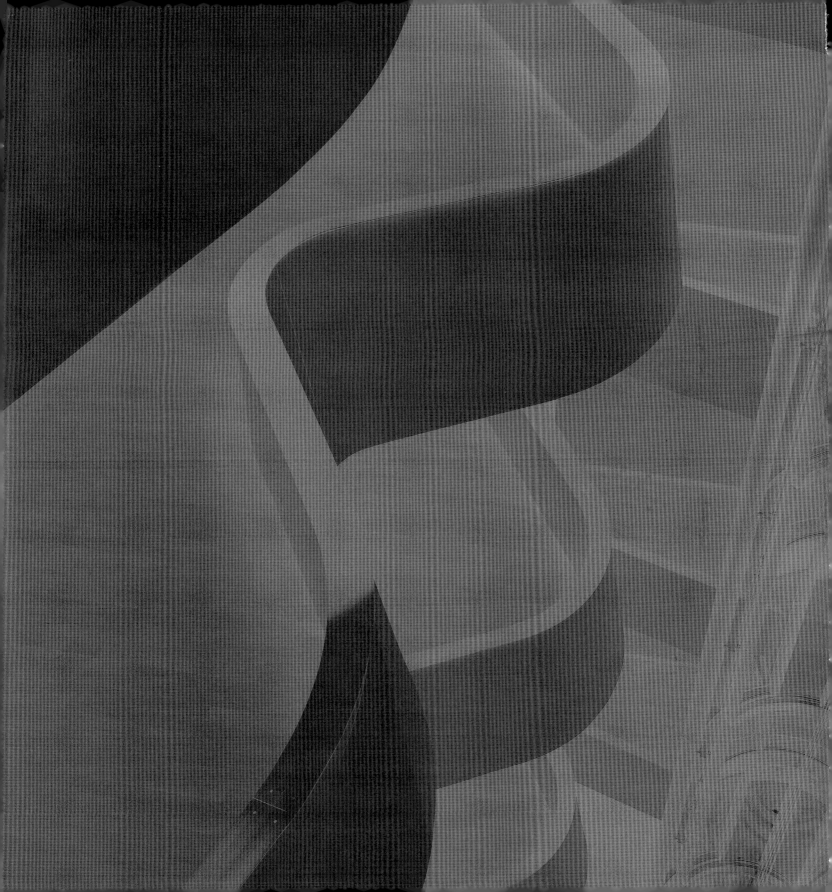

y Worldwide Headquarters

Armstrong, Inc. Headquarters
Philadelphia, Pennsylvania

Drexel University Residence
Philadelphia, Pennsylvania

Concordia Lutheran College Campus
Ann Arbor, Michigan

Municipal Services Building
Philadelphia, Pennsylvania

Randolph-Macon
Ashland, Virginia

American Baptist Convention Headquarters
Valley Forge, Pennsylvania

E.I. DuPont de Nemours & Co. Headq
Wilmington, Delaware

1 Academy Christ Chapel
Pennsylvania

Triangle Publication, Inc. WFIL Broadcasting Studios
Philadelphia, Pennsylvania

University of Pennsylvania Annenberg
Philadelphia, Pennsylvania

| 60 | 61 | 62 | 63 | 64 | 65 | 66 | 67 | 68 | 69 | 70 | 71 | 72 |

Three Thirty (330) Beacon St. Apartments
Boston, Massachusetts

State Street Bank Building
Boston, Massachusetts

Princeton University Jadwin
Princeton, New Jersey

United States Legation
Tangiers, Morocco

WGBH Studios
Boston, Massachusetts

Museum of Fine Arts Additions
Boston, Massachusetts

Veterans Stadium
Philadelphia, Pennsyl

World Health Organization Headquarters Competition
Geneva, Switzerland

Tabor A
Marion, M

Harvard University, LOEB Drama Center
Cambridge, Massachusetts

University of Massachusetts Student Life Building
Amherst, Massachusetts

ELEMENTS

Kling Architecture Founded
Founded by Vincent G. Kling, FAIA in Philadelphia, Pennsylvania

Phoenixville Hospital
Phoenixville, Pennsylvania

Monsanto Compar
St. Louis, Missouri

Peaslee Beach House
Mantoloking, New Jersey

Lankenau Hospital
Overbrook, Pennsylvania

Institute for Cancer Research
Fox Chase, Pennsylvania

Radio Corporation of America (RCA)
Cherry Hill, New Jersey

Earlham College Master Plan and Five Buildings
Richmond, Indiana

Episcopa
Overbrook

KLING

46   47   48   49   50   51   52   53   54   55   56   57   58   59

STUBBINS

Stubbins Architecture Founded
Founded by Hugh A. Stubbins, FAIA in Cambridge, Massachusetts

Berlin Congress Ha
Berlin, Germany

Weston Country School
Weston, Massachusetts

Sharpe House
Pojac Point, Rhode Island

Chelsea Veterans Housing
Chelsea, Massachusetts

New Haven Redevelopment
New Haven, Connecticut

Broadmeadow Elementary School
Needham, Massachusetts

ELEMENTS

Fund Society Headquarters
a

Bell Atlantic Tower
Philadelphia, Pennsylvania

Penn State University US Navy Applied Research Lab
State College, Pennsylvania

poration 11 Penn Center
Pennsylvania

Merrill Lynch & Co. Corporate Campus
Princeton, New Jersey

Prudential Property Regional Headquarters
Roseland, New Jersey

National Institutes of Health Child Health and Neurosciences Center
Bethesda, Maryland

Drexel University Engineering Center
Philadelphia, Pennsylvania

GlaxoSmithKline Medicines Research Centre
Stevenage, United Kingdom

88   89   90   91   92   93   94   95   96

Bank One Building
Indianapolis, Indiana

Landmark Tower – Minato Mirai 21
Yokohama, Japan

Building

The Ronald Reagan Presidential Library
Simi Valley, California

Vanderbilt University Psychology Building
Nashville, Tennessee

University of Chicago Sciences Learning Center
Chicago, Illinois

Singapore Treasury Building
Singapore

Duke University, Neurosciences Research Laboratory
Durham, North Carolina

University of Connecticut Health Center
Farmington, Connecticut

Philadelphia Saving:
Philadelphia, Pennsylvar

en's College Chapel

AT&T Corporate Headquarters
Basking Ridge, New Jersey

Villanova University, Connelly Center
Villanova, Pennsylvania

Radnor C
Philadelphia

Bell Telephone Laboratories
Murray Hill, New Jersey

Scheie Eye Institute
Philadelphia, Pennsylvania

Cargill Inc.
Minnetonka, Minnesota

ming Arts Center

International Monetary Fund Headquarters
Washington, District of Columbia

Community College of Philadelphia
Philadelphia, Pennsylvania

| 74 | 75 | 76 | 77 | 78 | 79 | 80 | 81 | 82 | 83 | 84 | 85 | 86 | 87 |

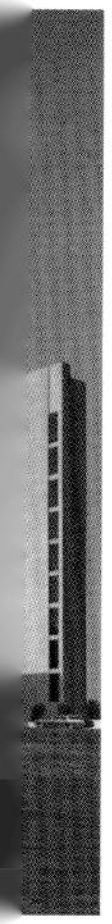

sics Lab

Citicorp Center
New York, New York

Pacwest
Portland, Oregon

RIT National Institute for the Deaf
Rochester, New York

Cornell University Biological Sciences
Ithaca, New York

Dade County Office
Miami, Florida

my, Academic Center
chusetts

Mount Holyoke College, Willits-Hallowell Center
South Hadley, Massachusetts

Harrah's Holiday Inn Casino
Atlantic City, New Jersey

Copley Place Marriott Hotel
Boston, Massachusetts

Federal Reserve Bank of Boston
Boston, Massachusetts

Carnegie Center
Princeton, New Jersey

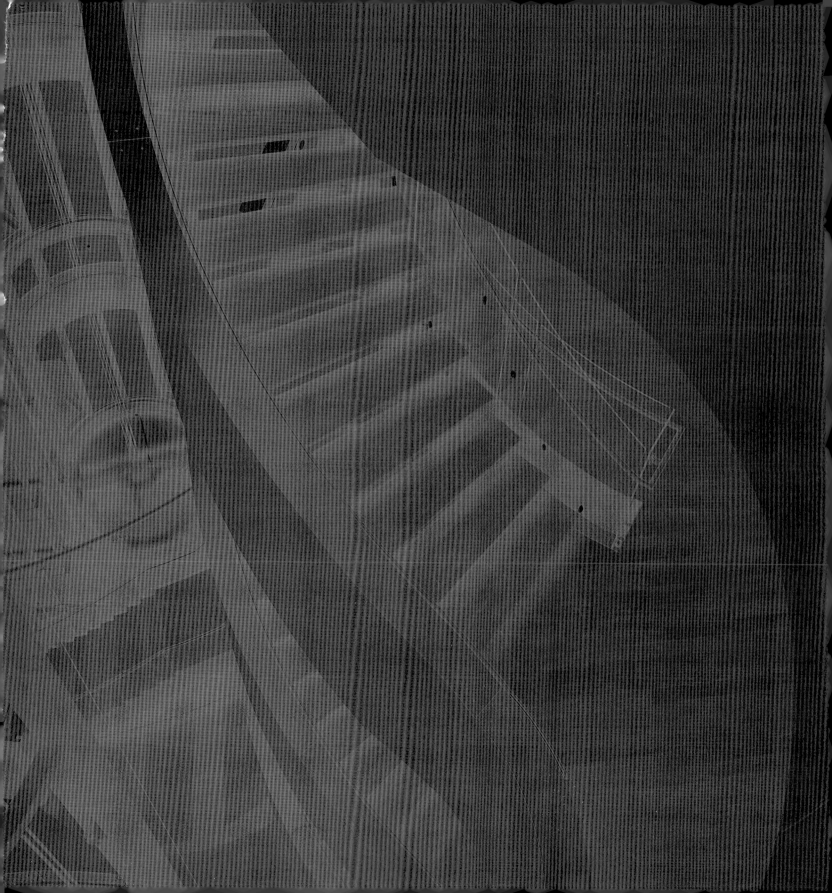

PEASLEE BEACH HOUSE

DESIGN / COMPLETION: 1942 / 1943
LOCATION: MANTOLOKING, NEW JERSEY
CLIENT: PEASLEE FAMILY
AREA: 2,200 SQUARE FEET (204 SQUARE METERS)

Set comfortably on a stretch of dunes between Barnegat Bay and the Atlantic Ocean, this beach house was designed by Vincent G. Kling while he was still a graduate student at M.I.T. and in collaboration with a very sympathetic pair of clients. Study of the project began with the familiar Colonial seaside schemes, which were discarded as they failed to meet the owners' requirements. The design that was finally adopted has an elevated living room that assures a better view and keeps sand and water out of the main part of the house. The open area at ground level provides a shady spot for resting and dining, with a kitchen adjacent. Bedrooms are placed a few steps above and are reached by a sheltered outside passage. Because of the special and rigorous climatic conditions in such a location, materials were selected with particular care: slate, tile, brick, wood, and plywood were used for the main structural and finishing materials.

Impressive as the exterior is in its freshness and vigor, the living room exemplifies the directness with which the solution was achieved. There are excellent views of both ocean and bay, and the general character of the room is in perfect harmony with the location and the requirements of use. The large windows are shaded by the fixed overhang in summer, but fully exposed to the winter sun; as the house is used for winter weekends, this provides a welcome supplement to the heating system.

This small house preceded, but greatly contributed to, the establishment of Vincent G. Kling and Associates and identified a commitment to Modernism that governed his work to follow. Within a few years of receiving recognition for this small residence, he was afforded the opportunity to design significant and complex facilities.

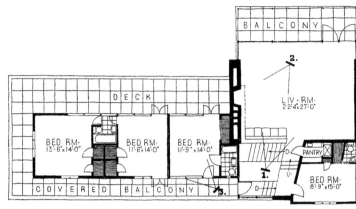

LANKENAU HOSPITAL

DESIGN / COMPLETION: 1950 / 1953
LOCATION: OVERBROOK, PENNSYLVANIA
CLIENT: LANKENAU HOSPITAL
AREA: 6,000,000 SQUARE FEET (557,000 SQUARE METERS)

Formerly known as the German Hospital of Philadelphia, Lankenau Hospital was chartered in 1860 to treat German immigrants. As the years passed, and as a matter of necessity, the hospital relocated from Philadelphia to Lower Merion in 1953. The Lankenau Hospital Board originally wanted to place Lankenau adjacent to Lancaster Avenue. The architect, Vincent G. Kling, convinced the Board that building a "hospital on the hill" would be more suitable, providing patients and employees with comforting views of open space.

This long-range development created a complete community health and medical research center on a large suburban site. Major elements included a basic hospital with 320 beds and support facilities that would eventually accommodate 500 beds, as well as a medical survey building with 126 beds, plus research, diagnostic, and therapy facilities. The master plan also encompassed medical offices, a medical and nursing school, and a geriatrics center on the 92-acre (37-hectare) suburban site.

The H-shaped plan of the hospital provides all patient rooms a southern orientation, a distant view, and protection from the noise emanating from both entrance and service courts. The large first floor encompasses community service areas including a health museum, public waiting rooms, a cafeteria, and open terrace.

The long, low character of the building mass is reinforced by ribbon windows, projecting bays, and a narrow, floating roof profile that helps integrate the form with its hilltop site. The low sills of the horizontal windows allow bed-ridden patients expansive views.

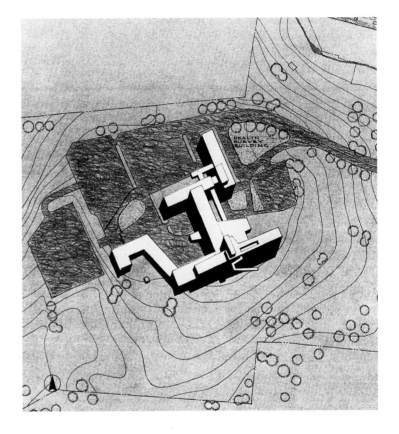

SHARPE HOUSE

DESIGN / COMPLETION: 1953 / 1955
LOCATION: POJAC POINT, RHODE ISLAND
CLIENT: HENRY D. SHARPE, JR.
AREA: 3,500 SQUARE FEET (325 SQUARE METERS)

The low, horizontal structure of the 1955 Sharpe House was merged with its setting of woodland and water by the use of post and beam to accommodate an almost entirely glass façade. Its pitched roof and staggered plan created an interplay of proportion, transparency, and expansiveness, making a structure symbolic of shelter.

Designed for a spit of wooded land projecting into a small lake, this family house is divided into distinct zones to allow privacy and freedom for individual as well as family activities, plus expansive space for entertaining. The two-story children's wing, separated by the entry from the rest of the house, has bedrooms over a workspace below. A link gives the master suite complete autonomy at one end of the plan. Both the master suite and the living room have wooden decks hovering over the ground and the water. The vestibule and dining room floors are marble with a Roman mosaic embedded in the hall.

The house makes dramatic use of fixed and sliding glass to exploit the surrounding water and trees. This quality of transparency, combined with the low profile, allows the house to blend with the landscape. In the two-level living and dining area, the wooden ceiling follows the pitch of the roof, enhancing the quality of space and interplay among volumes.

This early residence typifies the economy of means, elegance of structure, and clear expression of function that are integral to the larger projects to follow.

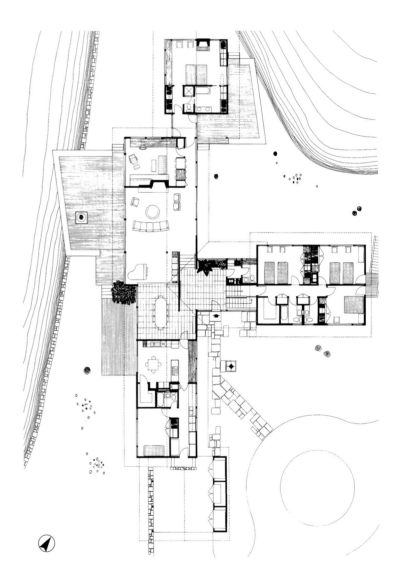

BERLIN CONGRESS HALL

DESIGN / COMPLETION: 1955 / 1957
LOCATION: BERLIN, GERMANY
CLIENT: BENJAMIN FRANKLIN FOUNDATION AND THE CITY OF BERLIN
AREA: 125,000 SQUARE FEET (11,600 SQUARE METERS)

The Congress Hall in Berlin has become a symbol of freedom of thought and creative expression. A gift from the United States Government, this international conference center is the embodiment of international goodwill and cultural exchange.

Designed as a new building type, with its daring catenary roof supported by large concrete arches, Congress Hall occupies a prominent 11-acre (4.5-hectare) level site near the center of Berlin, bounded by the Tiergarten and the River Spree. The 125,000-square-foot (11,600-square-meter) structure consists of two elements integrated into a single architectural expression. A 1,200-seat auditorium, equipped with multi-lingual translation facilities, is the dominant feature, with supporting exhibition rooms, offices, committee rooms, and restaurants surrounding the lower levels.

To accentuate the dominance of the main hall, the site was given a gentle upward slope around the building. The monumental arches continue the upward movement of the sloped site and rise to shelter the auditorium walls and support the roof. The distinctive shape of the auditorium roof, set upon its rectangular plaza, was intended to communicate a message of future promise.

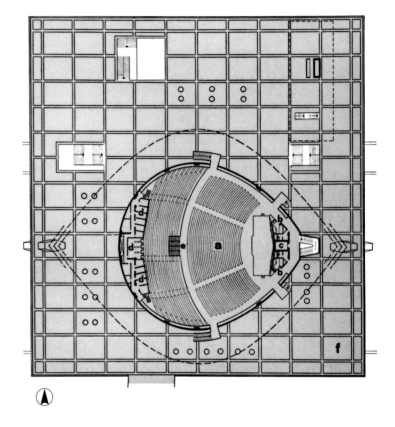

MUNICIPAL SERVICES BUILDING

DESIGN / COMPLETION: 1960 / 1965
LOCATION: PHILADELPHIA, PENNSYLVANIA
CLIENT: CITY OF PHILADELPHIA
AREA: 500,000 SQUARE FEET (46,500 SQUARE METERS)

Located in the heart of Center City Philadelphia, adjacent to City Hall, the Municipal Services Building was designed to streamline the various administrative functions servicing the public in a centralized location. Throughout the years, the expanding municipal government had outgrown the offices in City Hall and City Hall Annex, resulting in additional costly leases of various commercial offices in downtown Philadelphia. In 1952, the Mayor recommended the construction of a new building in Reyburn Plaza to accommodate the need for additional offices. The Municipal Services Building, as expressed by Vincent G. Kling, "reflects the important image of a new and dynamic City Government bringing great progress to Philadelphia. Surrounded by light, the building is a powerful yet elegant symbol of its public ownership."

For both aesthetic and functional purposes, the Municipal Services Building's elemental form is that of a symmetrical Greek cross. The cruciform plan accentuates the building's sense of verticality and dignity. The building's four wings create flexibility in serving a variety of office functions, and the inward corners of the cruciform allow for the windows to reach close to the core, maximizing the amount of sunlight exposure in all of the offices. The design filters the most public activities into a great public service concourse below street level, where citizens enjoy direct access to the building from public transit and the nearby Penn Center Concourse without having to cross busy streets. The remaining offices are grouped in a 16-story tower rising 264 feet (80 meters) above the plaza and occupying only 25 percent of the site, leaving most of the square open for a civic plaza enhanced with colored granite slabs, greenery, and decorative sculptures.

The omni-directional tower is enclosed with specially designed, granite-faced, precast window panels, using a new construction technique developed particularly for this building. The precast units were designed to accommodate a unique "sandwich" window, consisting of two panes of glass 5 inches (13 centimeters) apart. The space in between the two panes serves as insulation and holds a built-in vertical blind, and the outer pane is tinted bronze to minimize the glare of the sun. The well-proportioned windows, granite-faced frames, and colored glass result in a façade that is rich with light and shadow patterns, serving as a proper complement to the traditional façades of the neighboring structures while remaining strikingly modern.

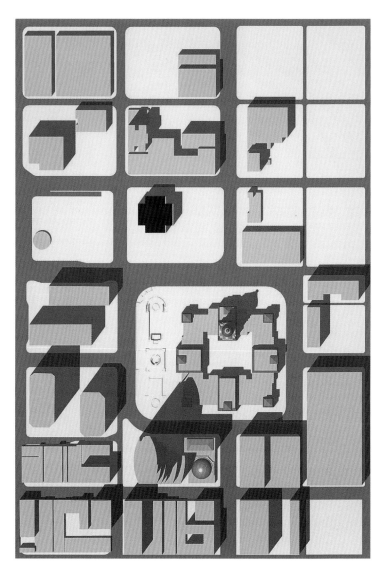

UNIVERSITY OF CONNECTICUT HEALTH CENTER

DESIGN / COMPLETION: 1967 / 1974
LOCATION: FARMINGTON, CONNECTICUT
CLIENT: UNIVERSITY OF CONNECTICUT
AREA: 1,100,000 SQUARE FEET (102,000 SQUARE METERS)

Vincent G. Kling envisioned a "cathedral of health" for the University of Connecticut Health Center, planning the campus facility on the top of a hill, much as a village church exists as a focal point for its community. A circular structure with angled windows and a central courtyard, the 1,100,000-square-foot (102,000-square-meter) health center is affiliated with the medical and dental schools and contains five major elements: a teaching wing, combining medical and dental degree programs with conference and seminar rooms and a 100,000-volume library; outpatient clinics for both medical and dental care, each able to accommodate 100,000 visits per year; a 200-bed hospital, which can expand to 400 beds; a research pavilion; and a behavioral research study facility.

Set within 162 acres (66 hectares) of wooded hilltop, the building commands views of the Hartford skyline 8 miles (13 kilometers) to the east. Designed to be "inspiring, soft, and approachable" in spite of its size, and the 7 miles (11 kilometers) of corridors linking its 2,000 rooms, the center is organized around a central courtyard providing not only a sense of place and orientation, but also an abundance of daylight. A lofty multi-level lobby and library open onto this planted courtyard providing a dramatic introduction to the facility.

The ten-story central curved spine houses comprehensive research activities including: chemistry, biochemistry, biology, microbiology, and physics laboratories. The organization of the programmatic elements was predicated on facilitating interrelationships among research, teaching, and patient care, with designed opportunities for communication among the many disciplines involved.

The concrete structure is punctuated with canted vertical windows that frame views while mitigating glare from the unusually wide range of solar orientation. Vertical circulation elements are expressed in counterpoint to the predominantly curved surface of the enclosure.

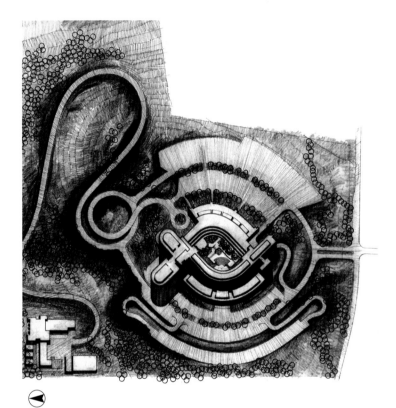

BELL LABORATORIES

DESIGN / COMPLETION: 1971 / 1974
LOCATION: MURRAY HILL, NEW JERSEY
CLIENT: BELL TELEPHONE LABORATORIES
AREA: 512,000 SQUARE FEET (47,600 SQUARE METERS)

A five-story administrative office and laboratory addition to the Bell Telephone Laboratories complex totaling 512,000 square feet (47,600 square meters) was designed to serve as the primary entrance to this major R&D campus. It is connected to the existing buildings on all levels to permit free circulation of personnel throughout the entire complex.

Creating a strong axial relationship between the new front door and administrative areas, and the research spaces beyond, the linear mass is fronted by a compressed pyramidal form that symbolizes its comparative importance, while engaging with the landscape. From a distance, the sloped roofs and strong chimney expression appears to be sympathetic to the surrounding residential development. Clad in a standing seam metal roof, and glass and masonry walls, the building form and envelope connote the technological focus of its internal program.

The headquarters include a cafeteria with seating for 1,300, a 30,000-volume library, exhibit areas, a conference/dining room accommodating 125 people, and lecture/training rooms. Executive offices and additional conference rooms are located on the uppermost floor.

Electronics research laboratories and offices were designed with movable partitions for maximum flexibility. The labs are backed up to a 6-foot-wide (2-meter) service corridor to permit mechanical service changes to keep abreast of developing technologies. The dry labs contain an 18,000-square-foot (1,700-square-meter) laminar airflow clean room.

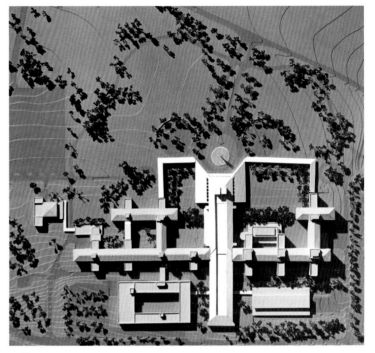

CITICORP CENTER

DESIGN / COMPLETION: 1973 / 1977
LOCATION: NEW YORK, NEW YORK
CLIENT: CITIBANK
AREA: 1,600,000 SQUARE FEET (149,000 SQUARE METERS)

A dramatic urban presence in New York City since its inception, Citicorp Center is a unique development combining an office tower, Saint Peter's Lutheran Church, retail shops, a public atrium, a pedestrian plaza, and a connection to the subway, on one site.

The tower, rising 914 feet (280 meters) from the street, is physically and visually one of the most significant buildings in Midtown. This sense of drama is enhanced by the crown of the building, which is sloped to the south and was anticipated to be used as a solar energy collector.

Bright aluminum and reflective glass enclose the 46 floors of the tower. In order to provide air, light, and space at the street level, the building is elevated on four 114-floor-high columns that support the tower at the midpoint of each façade, cantilevering the corners, and enabling the pedestrian functions of plaza, church, retail areas, building lobbies, subway entry, and galleria to nestle around the base of the tower.

Technological innovation is significant. Diagonal bracing, clear-span floors, and the first use of a tuned mass damper to moderate building motion are aspects of the unique structural design. A heat reclamation system, custom-designed low-brightness lighting, a computer-based building management system, and double-deck elevators are important elements of energy conservation, and quite innovative for their time.

Contrasting the smooth skin and technological precision of the office tower, the rough-hewn granite exterior of St. Peter's gives the church a distinct identity. A modern abstraction, evoking simplicity and dignity, the church and adjacent plaza enhance the pedestrian environment, as the tower's presence contributes to the city as a whole.

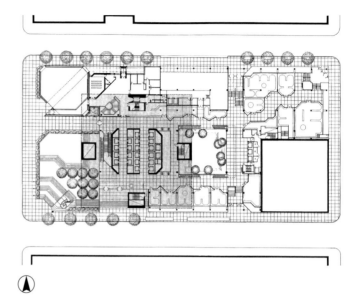

Citicorp Center

Citicorp Center

FEDERAL RESERVE BANK OF BOSTON

DESIGN / COMPLETION: 1972 / 1977
LOCATION: BOSTON, MASSACHUSETTS
CLIENT: FEDERAL RESERVE BANK OF BOSTON
AREA: 1,138,000 SQUARE FEET (106,000 SQUARE METERS)

Three main influences converged to shape this design: the importance of a clear expression of public and private functions within a unified scheme, the need for well-defined circulation, and the requirement for a high level of security. Project requirements included maximum-security areas for coin, currency, and check operations; a major banking floor; space for executive and administrative functions; employee facilities; and rentable space for future expansion.

The solution places the secure and banking operations, which require large areas, in a separate low-rise block and the office floors in a high-rise tower offering views over the harbor. To integrate the two elements, a connecting link was designed to accommodate employee facilities, a public gallery/display area, and a central control station strategically located with an overall view of the complex. At ground level, a 419-seat auditorium is available for public concerts or lectures. The employee cafeteria at the top of the low-rise building has the added amenity of a landscaped roof garden.

To provide open, flexible office floors, service cores were located at each end of the tower instead of in the middle, providing for large clear spans of column-free space. Continuous uninterrupted glass walls were achieved by freeing the columns from the exterior walls. Outside and above the glass, projecting aluminum spandrels serve as sunshades to shield the windows from glare in the summer yet allow the sun to reach the glass in winter. The mullion-free, butt-glazed outer wall surfaces permit the placement of partitions at any point, thus increasing flexibility of the space.

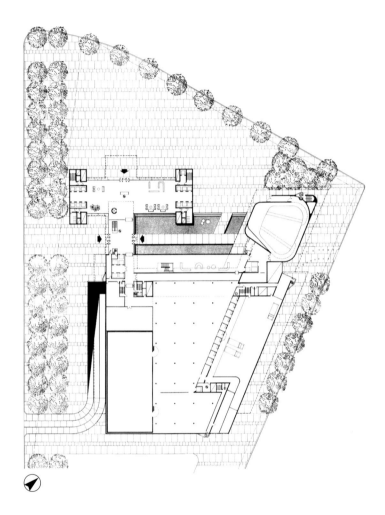

Federal Reserve Bank of Boston

DREXEL UNIVERSITY ENGINEERING CENTER

DESIGN / COMPLETION: 1988 / 1991
LOCATION: PHILADELPHIA, PENNSYLVANIA
CLIENT: DREXEL UNIVERSITY
SQUARE FOOTAGE: PHASE I – 68,000 SQUARE FEET (6,300 SQUARE METERS) / PHASE II – 58,000 SQUARE FEET (5,400 SQUARE METERS)

This award-winning engineering center project has two notably successful aspects: it gives Drexel University a gateway to the campus for the first time in its more than 100-year history, and it celebrates Drexel's strength and reputation in contemporary engineering research. The use of bright terra-cotta brick reflects the color and material utilized throughout Drexel's campus (as distinguished from the darker brick of the adjacent University of Pennsylvania campus). Glazing with steel mullions and exposed ducts and vent stacks communicate and dramatize the presence of high technology.

Although a relatively modestly sized facility of 126,000 square feet (11,700 square meters), the two-building complex is packed with a variety of labs for high-technology research: ceramics, composite material, robotics, photolithography, biosensor, and catalysis and reaction engineering. A secured area designed to support behavioral simulation work is located in the basement.

The design placed all laboratories facing the street where pedestrians can look in on the facilities, equipment, and activities. Faculty offices and student spaces are grouped around an interior landscaped courtyard, which provides sheltered exposure for interaction and contemplation. The building mass around this popular courtyard is stepped to maximize solar penetration. Constantly alive with pedestrians, the sequence of entry events from Market Street, Philadelphia's major east–west artery, through an arcaded portal to the sun-drenched courtyard embodies the true meaning of experiencing architecture.

The 68,000-square-foot (6,300-square-meter) Bennett S. LeBow Engineering Center includes: 16,000 square feet (1,500 square meters) for materials engineering; a 14,000-square-foot (1,300-square-meter) specialty research center; CADD and other computer facilities; and 5,600 square feet (520 square meters) of classrooms, offices, and various support systems.

The Center for Automation Technology is a 58,000-square-foot (5,400-square-meter), five-story building functioning both as a flexible research laboratory and as an area for demonstrating ongoing research from 19 different laboratories on campus. Additionally, the building houses an integrated automation suite with a manufacturing test cell, biochemical engineering, catalysis and reaction engineering laboratories, and semiconductor engineering with clean rooms.

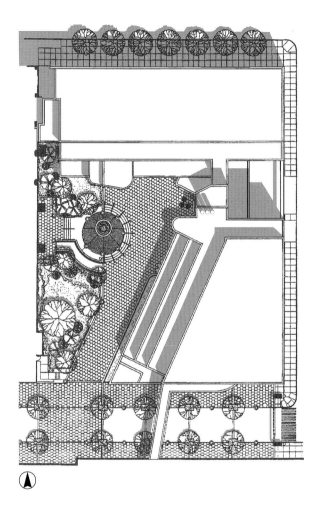

THE RONALD REAGAN PRESIDENTIAL LIBRARY

DESIGN / COMPLETION: 1988 / 1991
LOCATION: SIMI VALLEY, CALIFORNIA
CLIENT: THE RONALD REAGAN PRESIDENTIAL FOUNDATION
AREA: 153,000 SQUARE FEET (14,200 SQUARE METERS)

The Ronald Reagan Presidential Library serves primarily as a scholarly resource for study and research in the history of the Reagan Presidency and as an archival repository for the personal and official papers of Ronald Reagan and his associates. Sited along a ridge in the foothills north of the Santa Monica Mountains with a view to the west of the Pacific Ocean, the complex also incorporates an exhibit gallery and a 300-seat multi-purpose room.

An informal yet balanced harmony permeates the complex. At the principal entrance and approach to the Library, a loggia with a main gateway leads into a 150-foot (46-meter), cloistered courtyard featuring a central fountain. Landscaped with live oaks and shrubs common to Southern California, this enclosure is symmetrical and stately, befitting the dignity of the Office of the President of the United States.

A palette of materials was selected to be compatible with the Southern California region. Buff-colored stucco faces the exterior walls; Spanish tile covers all roofs; and Mexican Saltillo tile enhances the arcade and lobby floors. Interior walls employ drywall, teak, and French limestone. Window frames and doors are wood. Landscaping in the courtyard and around the building also employs native materials. The remainder of the 100-acre (40-hectare) site is left in its natural state.

Sympathetic to its region and climate and functional in plan, the Ronald Reagan Presidential Library is distinguished by its carefully integrated architecture and by its reflection of the spirit of the man whose Presidential papers are preserved here.

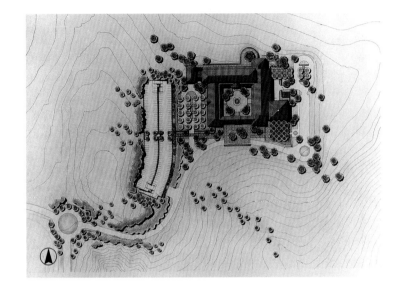

BELL ATLANTIC TOWER

DESIGN / COMPLETION: 1987 / 1991
LOCATION: PHILADELPHIA, PENNSYLVANIA
CLIENT: BELL ATLANTIC PROPERTIES
AREA: 1,370,000 SQUARE FEET (127,000 SQUARE METERS)

Within the orthogonal grid of Philadelphia, the grand diagonal of the Benjamin Franklin Parkway is important not only as a vehicular and pedestrian boulevard but also as a primary urban vista. The 1,370,000-square-foot (127,000-square-meter), 53-story Bell Atlantic Tower is set in front of Logan Circle, the heart of the Parkway, and is a major presence in the city's skyline.

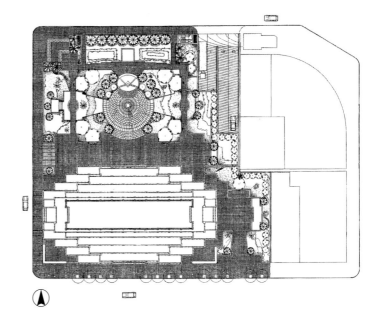

The principal challenges were to create a high-profile corporate presence for Bell Atlantic while honoring the covenants of city zoning ordinances, rightfully protective of the esteemed location. Setbacks required for buildings of this height of 230 feet (70 meters) from the centerline of the parkway contributed to the genesis of the design, coupled with an overriding awareness of the context. Resolution entailed massing the building to the south of the site, with an elegant urban plaza extending out to the parkway and the landscaped fountain of Logan Circle. Thus, the south and west faces of the tower continue the strong street edge which typifies the city's fabric. The plaza and park also work to bridge the two urban contexts.

The massing acknowledges the architectural traditions of the area while providing a singular identity for the corporate owner. Imperial red granite from Sweden was used to recall and honor the brick so prevalent throughout Philadelphia's history, and the plaza continues the fabric of urban parks interlaced throughout the city.

The building is stepped back at the top to heighten its verticality and to create terraces; at night, the crown is lit to create a waterfall of light against the sky. The faceted design provides a high percentage of perimeter area, and full-height office windows frame spectacular views of the city.

The 45,000-square-foot (4,200-square-meter) granite-paved pedestrian plaza features a circular reflecting fountain that provides a transition between the Benjamin Franklin Parkway and the building's entrance. A monumental three-story glass portal framed in granite extends into the interior public areas. The double-height lobby features polychrome marble walls and floors, accented with polished and satin bronze.

The Bell Atlantic Tower's form and surfaces were to convey not only an aura of stateliness, contributing to the building's inhabitants, but appropriateness to the architectural traditions of Philadelphia. Within a cityscape recently growing dense with cool, glass objects, the granite-clad design was to embody dignity.

Bell Atlantic Tower

LANDMARK TOWER – MINATO MIRAI 21

DESIGN / COMPLETION: 1990 / 1993
LOCATION: YOKOHAMA, JAPAN
CLIENT: MITSUBISHI ESTATE COMPANY, LTD.
AREA: 4,600,000 SQUARE FEET (427,000 SQUARE METERS)

Synthesizing Oriental sensibility with contemporary technology, the elegantly tapered Landmark Tower is the focal point of Minato Mirai 21 at the portal harborfront of Yokohama, Japan. Developed as the first phase of a 4,600,000-square-foot (427,000-square-meter) megastructure, the 75-story, 970-foot-high (295-meter) skyscraper is the tallest building in Japan.

Formerly a shipyard for Mitsubishi Heavy Industries, the 409,000-square-foot (38,000-square-meter) site is the symbolic and physical gateway to the coastal district that is being redeveloped by the Yokohama municipal government. An undertaking of unprecedented scale and density, the city's plan proposes a new port that is centered on business, culture, and commerce in a mix of private and public concerns.

Terraced and set back from the waterfront on its site, this office-hotel tower shares the open space with the Nippon Maru Park and Maritime Museum at its southern base, where two of its feet touch ground level. A fountain to the northeast of the tower marks the axial relationship of the structure, while the remaining portion of the open space includes walkways leading to shopping areas and landscaped areas of trees, hedges, and grass.

Combined in form as one distinctive building, the tower includes 1,560,000 square feet (145,000 square meters) of office space on 52 floors and 495,100 square feet (46,000 square meters) of hotel space on the top 15 floors of the tower. Uppermost hotel floors are projected out to accommodate two restaurants and an observation deck with a panoramic view to the Pacific Ocean, Mt. Fuji, and Tokyo. A skylit swimming pool and health facilities are located at the base of the hotel portion where it is recessed over the office floors. Other hotel facilities such as lobby, banquet, and reception rooms occupy the lower four floors in the retail block.

Rising above the complex, the steel and concrete Landmark structure is clad in a light-hued granite. Conceived as a strong solid vessel that is chiseled with a delicate core, the tower's ornamental treatment and origami-like folded plate evoke Japanese traditions. Like the teeth of oriental combs, the building's windows interlock with its structural elements. Like a huge Japanese lantern, uplit at night at the top four chamfered corners and in its hotel center, Landmark Tower serves as a lighthouse beacon to the new Yokohama and its rising future.

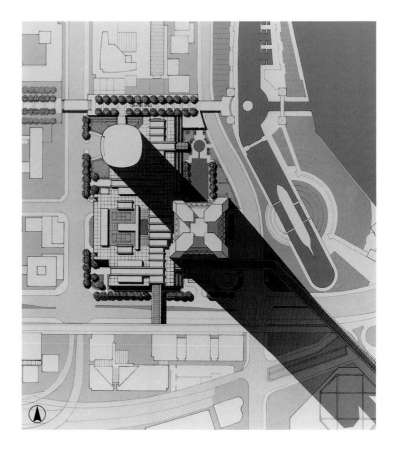

Landmark Tower – Minato Mirai 21

GLAXOSMITHKLINE MEDICINES RESEARCH CENTRE

DESIGN / COMPLETION: 1993 / 1995
LOCATION: STEVENAGE, UNITED KINGDOM
CLIENT: GLAXOSMITHKLINE
AREA: 1,760,000 SQUARE FEET (163,200 SQUARE METERS)

This 1,760,000-square-foot (163,200-square-meter), state-of-the-art research laboratory and office program on a 74-acre (30-hectare) campus is composed of twelve four- to six-story structures and two three- and four-level garages that are master planned to form a highly interactive campus enhanced by greens, ponds, and water features. The objective was to create a quality work environment worthy of world-class scientists and professionals and, at the same time, encourage a close-knit community.

The semi-rural setting of a project of this size and program required landscaped areas to soften its presence. The main research and administrative buildings are arranged around a central courtyard with the main entrance facing a water meadow that was developed into a lake. Approached over a pedestrian bridge from the visitor parking area, the four-story administrative building includes a conference center with a 200-seat lecture theater, seminar room facilities, and library; a cafeteria and restaurant; and occupational health and safety functions.

Within the complex, the system of circulation and activities is readily identifiable, providing a logical progression from the entrance and lobby to specialized research areas beyond. Each research building is unique, with differing widths and relationships to windows as appropriate to the functions of the laboratories and offices within.

The multiple research buildings are linked to one another via all-weather, covered pedestrian bridges—each flanked with multi-floor communications nodes composed of stairways, elevators, and informal seating and small conference areas. The 3,000 people of this small "city" are thereby encouraged to encounter and communicate with each other as part of an interactive and productive workplace that promotes interdisciplinary cooperation. Necessary separation and isolation are also provided for specialized laboratories and research areas, while modular lab design is utilized to accommodate layout changes easily and efficiently.

The relatively narrow buildings provide daylight and views for all occupied spaces except where lab activity requires otherwise. Close proximity of buildings required contamination prevention between intakes and exhausts, which had a marked effect on building mass relationships, the façade, and roof profile designs.

Queen Elizabeth II officially opened the Research Centre on April 19, 1995.

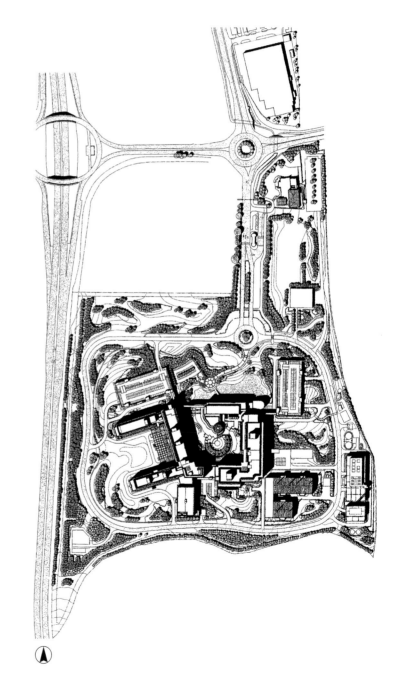

99 00

EVOLUTION

KLING

96

97

98

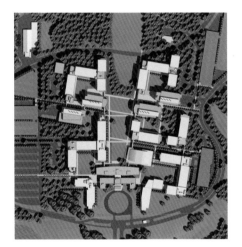

STUBBINS

EVOLUTION

04

05

01

02

03

US AMBASSADOR'S RESIDENCE AND CHANCERY BUILDING

DESIGN / COMPLETION: 1993 / 1996
LOCATION: SINGAPORE
CLIENT: U.S. DEPARTMENT OF STATE OVERSEAS BUILDINGS OPERATIONS
AREA: AMBASSADOR'S RESIDENCE: 10,000 SQUARE FEET (930 SQUARE METERS) / CHANCERY BUILDING: 115,000 SQUARE FEET (10,700 SQUARE METERS)

The U.S. Embassy in Singapore is composed of two separate buildings, the Chancery and an Embassy Mission Residence. The Chancery building is a 115,000-square-foot (10,700-square-meter) office building located in the heart of the garden district of Singapore. The design features a formal courtyard defining the building entry and a landscaped colonnade providing covered access from the site entrance to main entry. The five-story structure fronts Napier Road, a busy urban parkway, and is flanked by the British and Australian High Commissions. In addition to Consular Services, a United States Information Services Library and Agricultural Trade Office, Marine Security Guard Quarters, and an adjacent swimming pool, the building houses conference facilities, a cafeteria, and offices for 200 staff.

The principal exterior materials are stone and metal. The base is green, rock face granite with accents of polished black and rainbow granite. The upper portion of the building is thermal white granite. Polished stainless steel is used on the window frames, and matte stainless steel on the pavilion roof. Stainless steel plus white and green marble are used in the interior public spaces.

Located on a 3-acre (1-hectare) site in the Leedon Park district, the Embassy Mission Residence is a 10,000-square-foot (930-square-meter) facility comprising a reception hall, parlor, formal dining room for 48 people, guest suite, and private family quarters as well as staff accommodations. The design of the residence accommodates a delicate balance of functions: public versus private, and ceremonial versus familial. The separation of private and public functions was achieved by vertical separation of family and formal spaces. Local stone, wood, brick, and roof tiles were employed to reflect the immediate residential context.

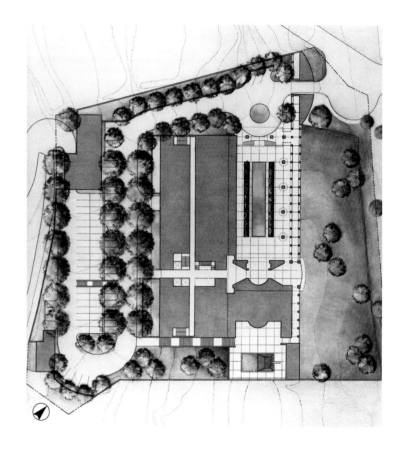

US Ambassador's Residence and Chancery Building

US Ambassador's Residence and Chancery Building

US FDA HEADQUARTERS CONSOLIDATION – MASTER PLAN

(IN ASSOCIATION WITH RTKL)

DESIGN / COMPLETION: 1997 / 2012
LOCATION: WHITE OAK, MARYLAND
CLIENT: GENERAL SERVICES ADMINISTRATION
AREA: 3,000,000 SQUARE FEET (279,000 SQUARE METERS)

In 1995, the Naval Ordnance Laboratory (NOL) in White Oak, Maryland was closed in accordance with the Defense Base Realignment and Closure Act. A year later, the site was acquired by the General Services Administration (GSA) to be developed into a new consolidated campus for the Food and Drug Administration (FDA). Despite their apparent disparity, these two facilities inhabiting a common site in succession represents continuity in purpose, reflecting the Federal Government's constant yet adaptive role in protecting the public.

Inscribed within the FDA master plan is an awareness of the site's history and continuity of purpose. While creating a new headquarters facility befitting the function and public identity of the FDA, the design preserves the historical significance of the NOL campus by incorporating its key building and maintaining the campus fabric. In the master plan, the historic Building One is transformed to become the focal point and main entrance for the FDA. The Centers of the FDA are organized around courtyards, providing a collegial atmosphere that encourages interaction between the more than 7,700 FDA employees. At the center of the campus, a grand commons visually orients the facility toward the impressive woodland that covers a large portion of the White Oak site. In order to preserve the natural wooded landscape and wetlands, the master plan concentrates building density so that it occupies only the previously developed portion of the site. By sensitively balancing the site's history, future, and environment, the design creates a place that is significant to both its users and the surrounding community.

The master plan is a product of thorough investigation of the site, context, and precedents. The design was informed by an in-depth study of campus precedents, of building typology, and of the historical events that transpired at the NOL. Careful attention was given to creating a pedestrian-scaled environment based on examples of successful public places. Extensive study was conducted to derive unique and creative security solutions necessary for a federal facility that will foster a sense of openness without compromising safety. Questions of sustainability have also fundamentally informed the design of the campus, buildings, and landscape.

The FDA campus is to be developed in multiple phases and is projected for completion in 2012.

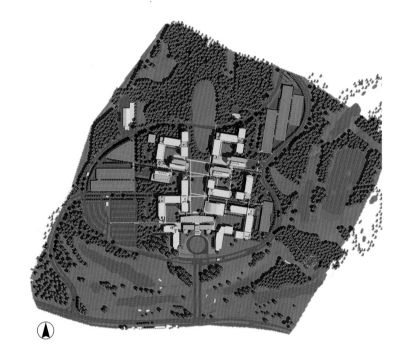

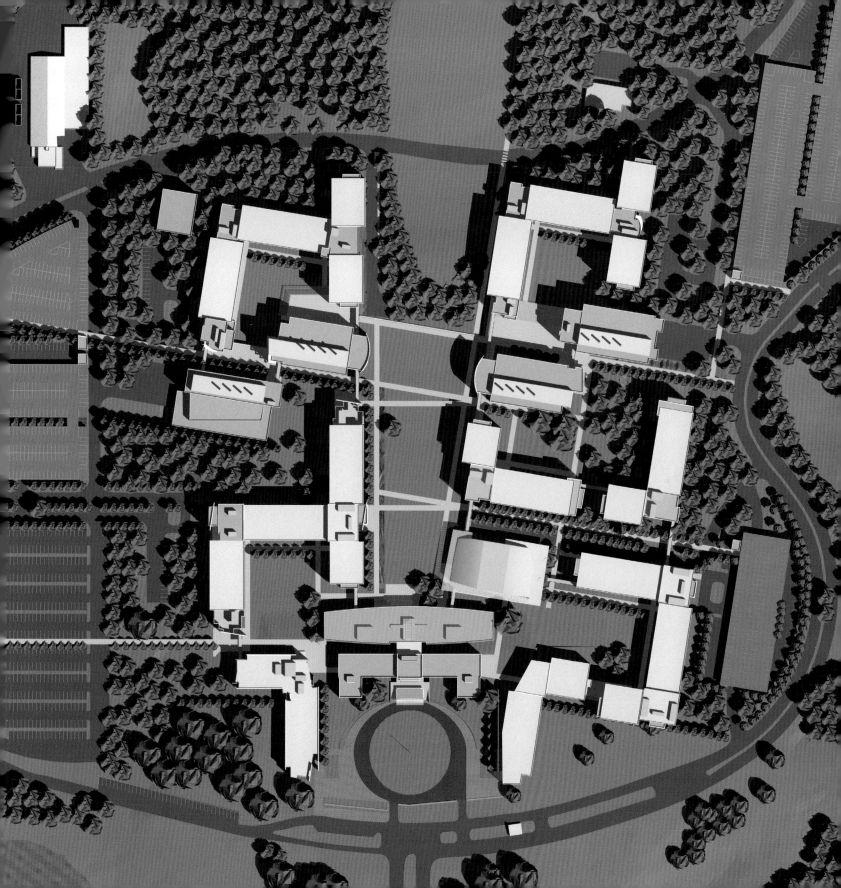

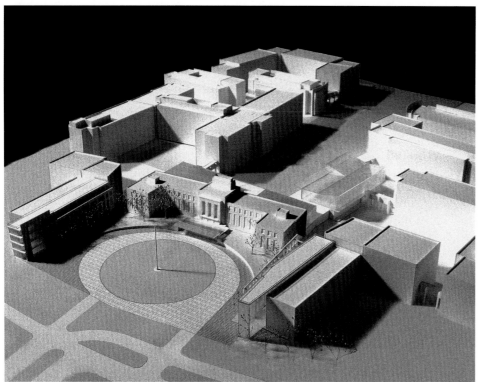

US FDA Headquarters Consolidation – Master Plan

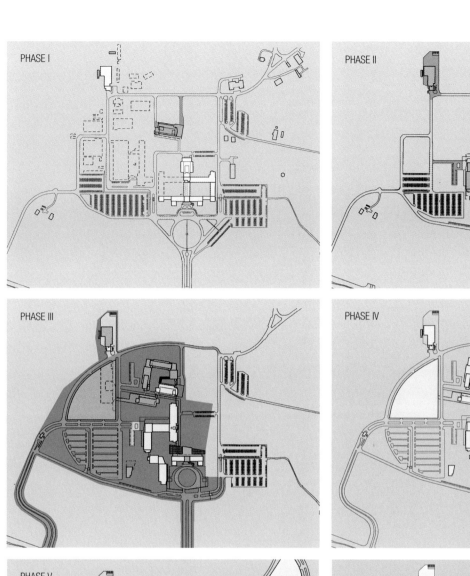

PHASE I

PHASE II

PHASE III

PHASE IV

PHASE V

DOW JONES & COMPANY BERNARD KILGORE CENTER

DESIGN / COMPLETION: 1996 / 1998
LOCATION: SOUTH BRUNSWICK, NEW JERSEY
CLIENT: DOW JONES & COMPANY, INC.
AREA: 450,000 SQUARE FEET (41,800 SQUARE METERS)

The design was created for an invited competition that required a master plan that focused on the addition of 900,000 square feet (83,600 square meters), and a first phase corporate office facility of 450,000 gross square feet (41,800 square meters) and parking for 1,200 cars. Challenges included incorporating the new large structure within a campus without the benefit of a plan for growth and linking this facility with four existing structures of diverse orientation and scale.

The building is designed to create a more cohesive campus while presenting the rotunda as a clear destination for people arriving from a main artery. The bridge across the main entry drive links the three easterly buildings and the on-grade connection to the information service building and provides sheltered access to the primary elements of the campus. The internal organization of the new facility responds to the issue of pedestrian traffic with a 700-foot-long (210-meter) grand avenue running along the long axis.

The architectural character directly responds to the existing context. Careful orchestration of massing components include parallel planes, volumes defined by seemingly discrete walls, a tripartite organization of the main office block, and the layering of forms balances the new building's scale with the existing very large and very small structures.

The Indiana limestone cladding was chosen for its responsiveness to the single existing limestone structure and the three existing precast-faced structures. The stone's coloration harmonizes with the various beige tones while its variegation further addresses the issue of scale. Clear glass windows are paired with horizontal and vertical solar control elements and are defined by custom extruded painted aluminum framing.

Issues inherent in creating an optimal open office environment—daylight, indirect lighting, efficiency, and flexibility—primarily condition the interior organization. The more public realm of this facility is incorporated within the first and basement floors and includes a fitness center, company store, café, and a gallery that is intended for changing exhibitions as well as for display of company artifacts.

The atrium is clad in green serpentine paving and is softened by bamboo. Cantilevered glass railings above and clear glass walls at the first floor describe its edges. The "wishbone" tracery that supports the skylight has been designed to not only glorify the space, but also to resolve seismic force requirements to tie the building halves together.

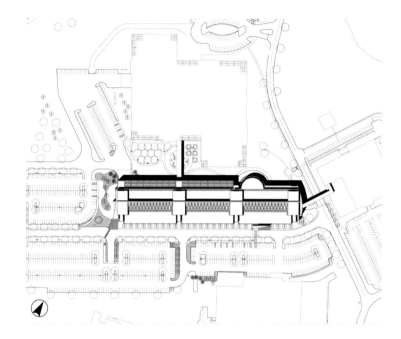

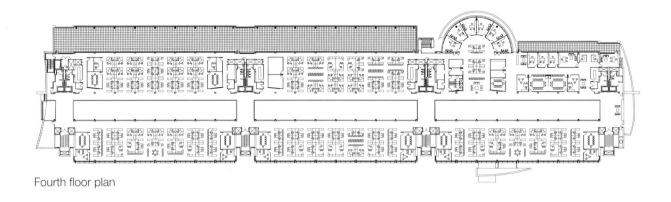

Fourth floor plan

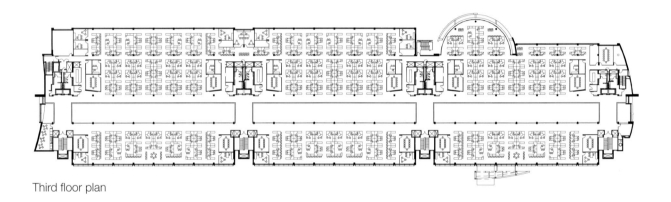

Third floor plan

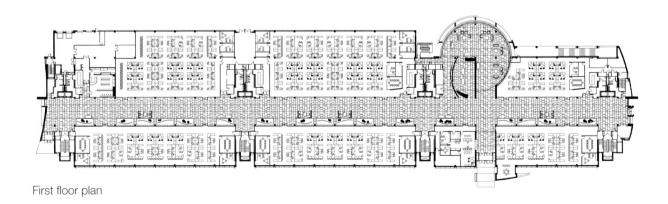

First floor plan

North elevation

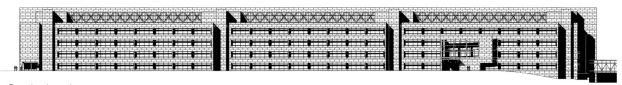

South elevation

East elevation

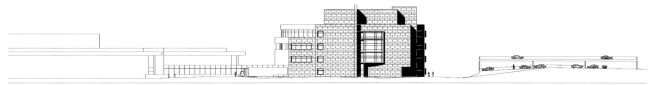

West elevation

Dow Jones & Company Bernard Kilgore Center

SAP NORTH AMERICAN HEADQUARTERS

DESIGN / COMPLETION: 1997 / 1999
LOCATION: NEWTOWN SQUARE, PENNSYLVANIA
CLIENT: SAP AMERICA, INC.
AREA: 400,000 SQUARE FEET (37,200 SQUARE METERS)

Located in a semi-rural suburb of Philadelphia, the 400,000-square-foot (37,200-square-meter) building accommodates 1,200 employees and up to 600 visitors to the demonstration and training centers that fulfill important functions for the company's products and services. The master plan includes a Phase II building of similar size and extension of the 1,000-car parking structure.

The building's role as a corporate headquarters demanded that the project present a distinctive image while its location required sensitivity to the farmland scale of the landscape and the small-town scale of its nearest neighboring buildings. Sited on the brow of a hill along a serpentine entry road, the building height yields to surrounding trees. The predominantly south-facing exterior wall of the 1,000-foot-long (305-meter) structure parallels a preexisting access road and curves so that the east end parallels nearby buildings. The transparent exterior of green tinted glass reflects and/or dissolves this highly geometric form into the texture, colors, and seasonal changes of the beautiful surrounding landscape.

The glass-enclosed entrance lobby, shared by employees and visitors alike, provides a clear orientation to the building's three main elements of traffic: controlled passage of employees to the office areas, trainees to training areas on the second floor, and prospective clients to the third floor. A 1,000- by 20-foot (305- by 6-meter) uninterrupted atrium along the north wall is the main street of the building. Open to each floor, it provides views of the landscaped courtyard and trees beyond through a 45-foot-high (14-meter) clear glass wall facing north.

The building has two wall systems: the aforementioned glass wall at the atrium predominantly to the north and a floor-to-ceiling curtain wall of blue-green glass predominantly to the south. In addition to allowing light and views into the building, the glass surfaces exploit the specific qualities of the material for the building's image within the landscape. Both walls are intended to provide a taut, continuous glass surface to the exterior. As such, the building is unabashedly object-like. Simultaneously, the thinness of the building and the transparency of its skin allow it to occasionally dematerialize within its context.

The design for the American Headquarters of the European-based computer software company is predicated on the dual issues of identity and respect for the environment. The building's character is deferential to the natural context while being expressive of technology and the readily visible dynamics of its workforce.

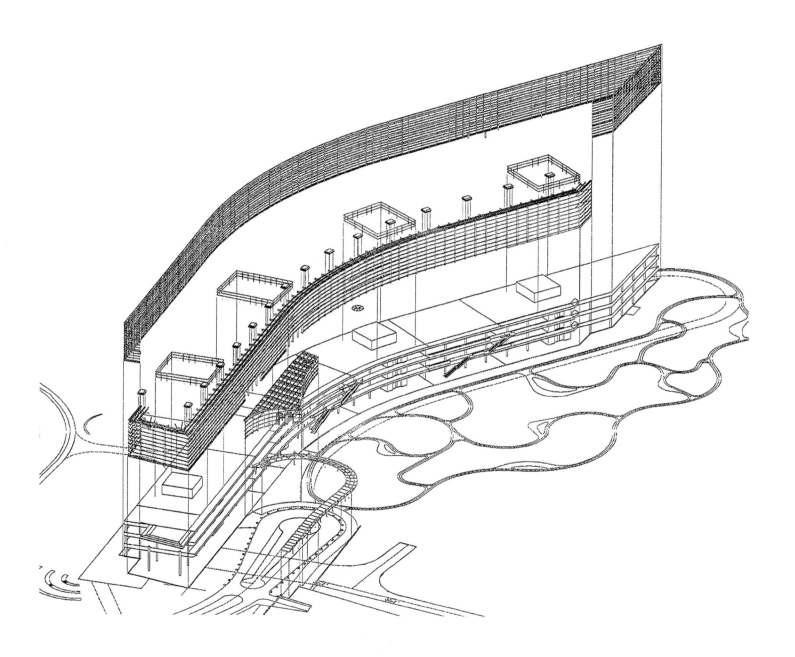

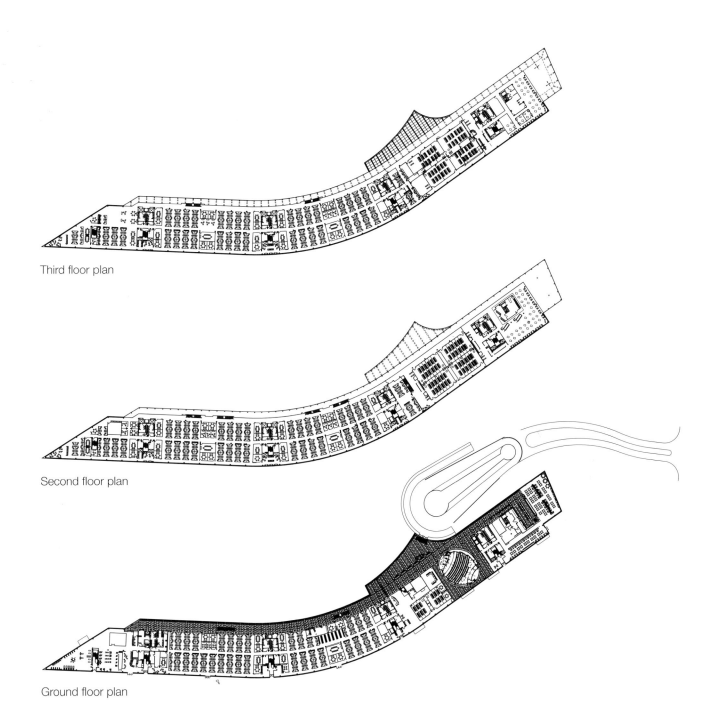

Third floor plan

Second floor plan

Ground floor plan

SAP North American Headquarters

SAP North American Headquarters

VENETIAN RESORT HOTEL CASINO

DESIGN / COMPLETION: VENETIAN: 1996 / 1999   VENEZIA: 2001 / 2003
LOCATION: LAS VEGAS, NEVADA
CLIENT: LAS VEGAS SANDS CORPORATION
AREA: 6,000,000 SQUARE FEET (557,000 SQUARE METERS)

The development of the Venetian took place during the "theme" phase in Las Vegas casino hotels. Immediately preceding it were the Bellagio (inspired by the picturesque town in the Como Lake district of Northern Italy), the Paris, and the Monte Carlo.

The Venetian, therefore, fit into the trend of using European icons for branding purposes. The ultimate success of these various properties was tied not to the connection made by visitors with the city of origin, but rather to the reinterpretation of its imagined characteristics into the overwrought panoply of the Las Vegas Strip.

In the case of the Venetian, its success as a themed destination resides in two components of its planning and execution: the Grand Canal Shoppes and the re-creation of St. Mark's Square.

The most powerful and symbolic character of Venice—its canals—are hidden within the Hotel and Casino development and used to lure visitors through a series of bridges and moving sidewalks to a second-level retail center. Here, gondolas ferry guests around 600,000 square feet (55,700 square meters) of high-end retail on a canal that meanders over the casino below. Above, a "sky ceiling" painted on an edge-lit vault creates the sensation of infinite depth, and separates the visitor from the realities of both time and place. After shopping or dining, guests descend escalators to arrive at the nexus of the Venetian's exposition and meeting facilities, its restaurants, and the back of its 100,000-square-foot (9,300-square-meter) casino, with no option but to transit back through the development's environs to the Strip or next destination.

The Strip identity of the Venetian is a stage-set of Venice's Grand Canal palaces and the Ca D'Oro, Rialto Bridge, Campanile, and Doge's Palace of St. Mark's Square—all recreated within five percent of actual scale. A team of artists overseen by a curator of Venetian antiquities produced highly accurate, measured drawings of the selected buildings from which thousands of latex molds were created. Into these molds an infinitely malleable cementitious material—Glass Fiber Reinforced Concrete—was cast, capturing in detail all of the stone carved arches and columns, trim pieces and capitals of Venice.

The 63-acre (25-hectare) site contains a 37-story hotel, a 5-acre (2-hectare) pool deck, and 2,500,000 square feet (232,000 square meters) of convention space. A second phase hotel, the Venezia, completed in 2003, added 1,000 additional luxury rooms to the 3,000 from Phase I, for a total of 4,000 all-suite hotel rooms.

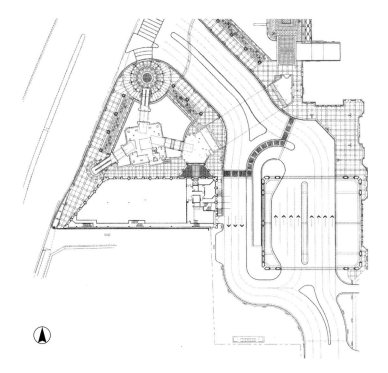

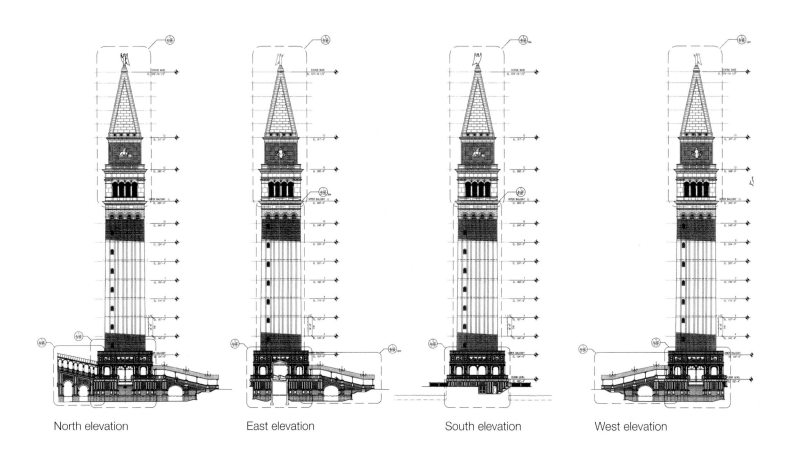

North elevation   East elevation   South elevation   West elevation

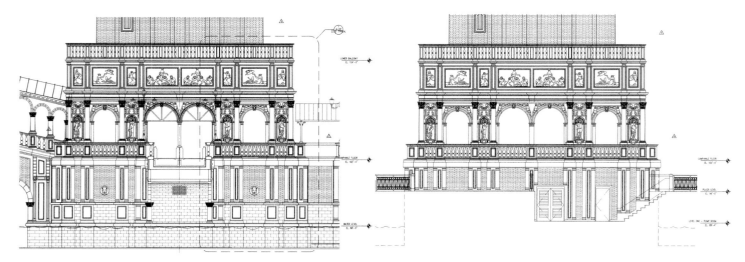

North campanile base elevation

South campanile base elevation

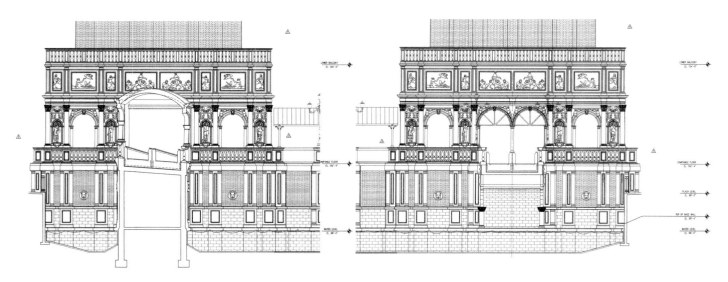

East campanile base elevation

West campanile base elevation

Venetian Resort Hotel Casino

Venetian Resort Hotel Casino

Venetian Resort Hotel Casino

DELMONICO STEAKHOUSE

(IN ASSOCIATION WITH HOLDEN & DUPUY FOR INTERIOR DESIGN)

DESIGN / COMPLETION: 1998 / 1999
LOCATION: LAS VEGAS, NEVADA
CLIENT: EMERIL LAGASSE
AREA: 15,000 SQUARE FEET (1,400 SQUARE METERS)

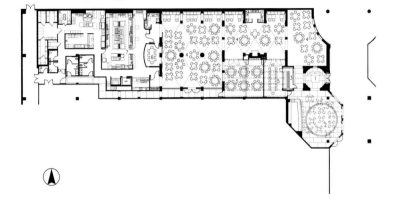

Delmonico Steakhouse was created by famed New Orleans restaurateur, Emeril Lagasse. Located on the ground floor of the Venetian Resort Hotel Casino, with convenient, enclosed access from the adjacent Sands Convention and Expo Center, some 375 patrons can be accommodated within its varied venues.

The design addresses the owner's request for a space with distinctive architectural character and scale that highlights a quiet and distinguished environment, complementing the quality of the menu, wine list, and service. The solution involves a play of minimal, modern interior elements against a simple, traditional architectural framework. Having drawn inspiration from the unadorned interiors of historic European basements, the main dining room has the character of a tasteful, stylish adaptation of a pre-existing space. Two smaller dining rooms have coffered wood ceilings and can be segregated and subdivided for private functions.

Entering the reception area through 12-foot-high (4-meter) oak doors, patrons are made aware of the high ceiling rotunda defining the bar, and a glass-enclosed, wooden-shelved wine collection that acts as an element of the processional to the dining areas beyond.

SHENZHEN CUSTOMS COMPLEX

DESIGN: 2000
LOCATION: SHENZHEN, CHINA
CLIENT: GOVERNMENT OF CHINA
AREA: 1,500,000 SQUARE FEET (139,000 SQUARE METERS)

The Chinese Bureau of Customs held an invitational competition for the design of its new complex to be located in the New Futian City Center in the technologically driven city of Shenzhen in southeastern China. The design of the complex is predicated on fulfilling the requirements of an efficient office environment, respecting and contributing to its siting, and representing the Customs Bureau in a manner both appropriate to its stature and endowed with the symbolism appropriate within its mission and the public understanding.

The 1,500,000-square-foot (139,000-square-meter) project includes a public customs processing facility along with private customs offices, training areas, a technology center, archives, reception rooms, recreational and dining facilities, auditorium, and a hotel. The composition of the entire complex allows each component to address its singular requirements within a cohesive whole. The office tower has been designed to create floor-by-floor environments that respond to the programmatic groupings and adjacencies while creating a workplace that affords broad views of the city and the adjacent mountains. The declaration hall and attendant support are configured to facilitate the processes involved within a carefully composed system of security zones.

At the completion of Phase I, the tower and linear bar give definition to the site: to the south as a backdrop to the public plaza and to signify entry; and to the east by creating an object which gives closure to and functions as an entrance to the City Center district. These two elements, moreover, pay close attention to the movement of vehicles and people from both public and private conveyances.

Surrounded by a free form glass-enclosed auditorium and restaurant, the 38-story tower is approached via a three-story atrium. A separate classroom, hotel, and recreational building cantilevers over the courtyard's amorphous reflecting pool. The careful play of interior and exterior space, form, and void respects the public versus private areas and their security issues while creating a unified landmark in the center of a bustling, pedestrian city.

The assemblage, which will ultimately define the complex, will have at its heart a cloister that is designed to permit the sharing of experience, but also protect the privacy of the Customs Bureau's employees. The north and west edges are designed in response to their internal functions, in a character sympathetic to the scale planned for the proximal blocks. The design is one of layers and layered meaning. It is expressive of edges, gateways, and most significantly, of passage.

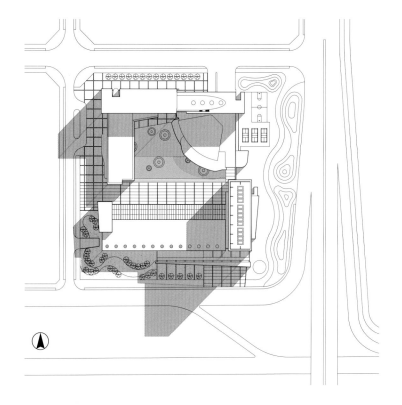

DATEK WORLD HEADQUARTERS

DESIGN / COMPLETION: 2001 / 2001
LOCATION: JERSEY CITY, NEW JERSEY
CLIENT: DATEK
AREA: 340,000 SQUARE FEET (31,600 SQUARE METERS)

The primary goal of the project was to provide a state-of-the-art headquarters for this high-technology software trading and online brokerage company. Challenges of the space included a diminutive base building floor plate with a disproportionately large and inefficient core, low floor-slab-to-floor-slab heights, irregular spacing of perimeter structural columns, and an aggressive 15-month schedule from design to occupancy. Within this space, Datek desired to combine five geographically distinct subsidiaries into one centralized location; create a new cultural identity; flatten its management hierarchy; achieve maximum flexibility and adaptability for the space; provide daylight and views to all workstations and offices; create opportunities for spontaneous and informal interaction; and raise the employee brand and marketing awareness.

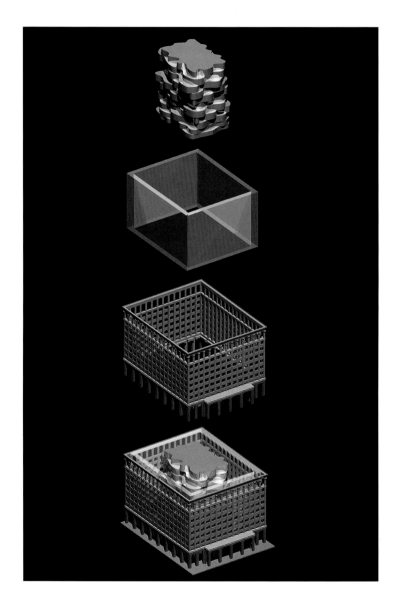

The design strives to embody the company's philosophy of transparency and egalitarianism. By situating all of the workstations and offices in a "systems zone" held back from the perimeter circulation corridor, natural light penetrates deep into the workspace, affording views of the Hudson River, Lower Manhattan, Ellis Island, and the Statue of Liberty. A scrim shade cloth assembly reduces solar heat gain while simultaneously providing uniform fenestration throughout the day and night. The systems zone is composed of demountable partitions, modular ceiling and lighting, and a raised floor system that gives the company a high degree of flexibility and efficiency to reconfigure the space as requirements change.

The design premise was an object-and-container relationship, developing formally and functionally interdependent elements and zones. The duality inherent in the design acts as a physical representation of the client's intertwined but distinct technological and financial components. An undulating vertical plane, or "morph" wall, surrounds the building service core and has dedicated spaces for a coffee bar, pantry, copy rooms, and various types of meeting areas on each of the office floors. The location of a major circulation area immediately outside this morph object defines the object as well as the boundary it provides between the outer spaces and the workstations and general office environment contained within the morph wall.

UNITED STATES POSTAL SERVICE MASTER PLAN

DESIGN: 2001
LOCATION: PHILADELPHIA, PENNSYLVANIA
CLIENT: KEATING BUILDING COMPANY
AREA: 14,000,000 SQUARE FEET (1,300,000 SQUARE METERS)

KlingStubbins was commissioned to execute master planning and design services, which included a fresh look at the redevelopment potential and scope of the United States Postal Service (USPS) properties from an architectural/engineering standpoint while continuing to gauge the potential site location in the broader redevelopment plans for Center City Philadelphia. KlingStubbins and its consultants proposed a redevelopment of the property, including plans and "vision pieces" that support Keating presentations to prospective tenants. The site's reuse options were evaluated with regard to its potential impact on the historic character of the Main Post Office building. Reuse alternatives are based on postal service requirements for continuing operation at the facility, development plans for the surrounding area, city zoning/redevelopment requirements, and community input. All proposed redevelopment was presented to interested parties, including, but not limited to, representatives of the USPS, Amtrak, the City of Philadelphia, local institutions, and prospective tenants.

A zoning analysis model was provided, as well as master planning for mixed-use development, such as entertainment, commercial/retail, educational, offices, hotel, and residential uses. The team also assessed the restoration of the existing postal facility's historic façade, including the implications for the Section 106 assessment. Conceptual architecture/engineering included structural, mechanical, and electrical engineering with evaluation of existing conditions in the three major buildings, building systems, structure, building shells, and connection to infrastructure.

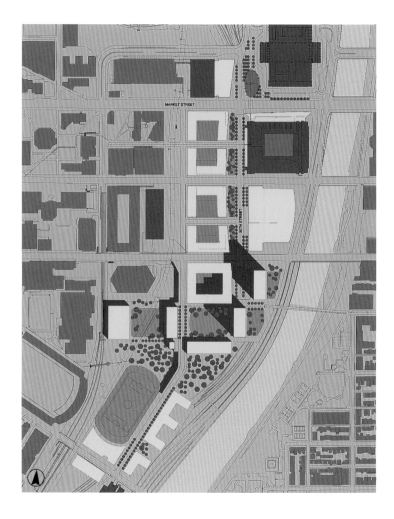

CENTER CITY TOWER

DESIGN: 2002
LOCATION: PHILADELPHIA, PENNSYLVANIA
CLIENT: COMCAST CORPORATION
AREA: 1,400,000 SQUARE FEET (130,000 SQUARE METERS)

One of Philadelphia's most important urban addresses was made available as a result of a fire that caused significant damage to a 1970s high-rise. The site is directly opposite City Hall and defined by a context of buildings that have existed for 30 years or longer. It is within these conditions, and with regard to the historical importance of the city's center, that these studies were executed.

The developed scheme is a stepped, softly curved 75-story tower. Intentionally designed to manifest an identity without direct reference to the site's history, the building is placed to mitigate the restrictive physical conditions that limit this particular city block—as both pedestrian-level experience and as an aspect of the city's skyline.

At grade, the plaza allows enhanced visual access south along Fifteenth Street, and more importantly, brings City Hall's Dilworth Plaza into a continuum of the urban fabric. This urban environment is also planned to provide a forecourt to the activity planned within the building's base, establishing much-needed public activity within the city's center. At the apex, the tower gradually evolves into a form separate from, but respectful of, the Beaux Arts spire that culminates the city government's home.

The total area of 1,400,000 square feet (130,000 square meters) is composed of floor plans ranging from 45,000 square feet (4,200 square meters) at the base to 6,000 square feet (560 square meters) at the top; a diversity that readily accommodates corporate functions ranging from broadcast studios and call centers to executive and conferencing areas; and that affords appropriate scale to the upper 12 condominium floors. Below-grade parking for 200 cars is provided without compromise to the very important underground concourse that ties the city's buildings and transportation links together.

Clad in clear and silk-screened vision glass, the building is intended to be seen as a highly identifiable, translucent object that is both a dominant and self-effacing element of this city's skyline—an element that even while passing from transparency to reflectivity continuously acts as a beacon celebrating Philadelphia's future.

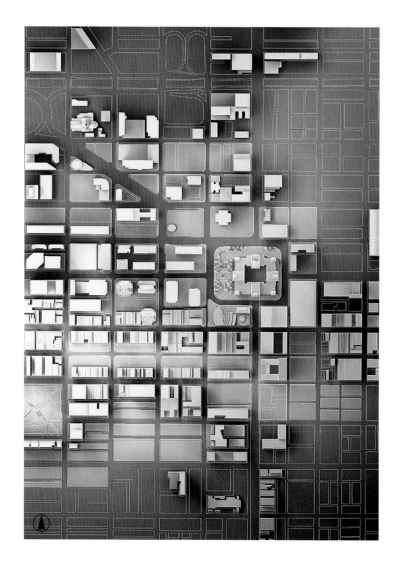

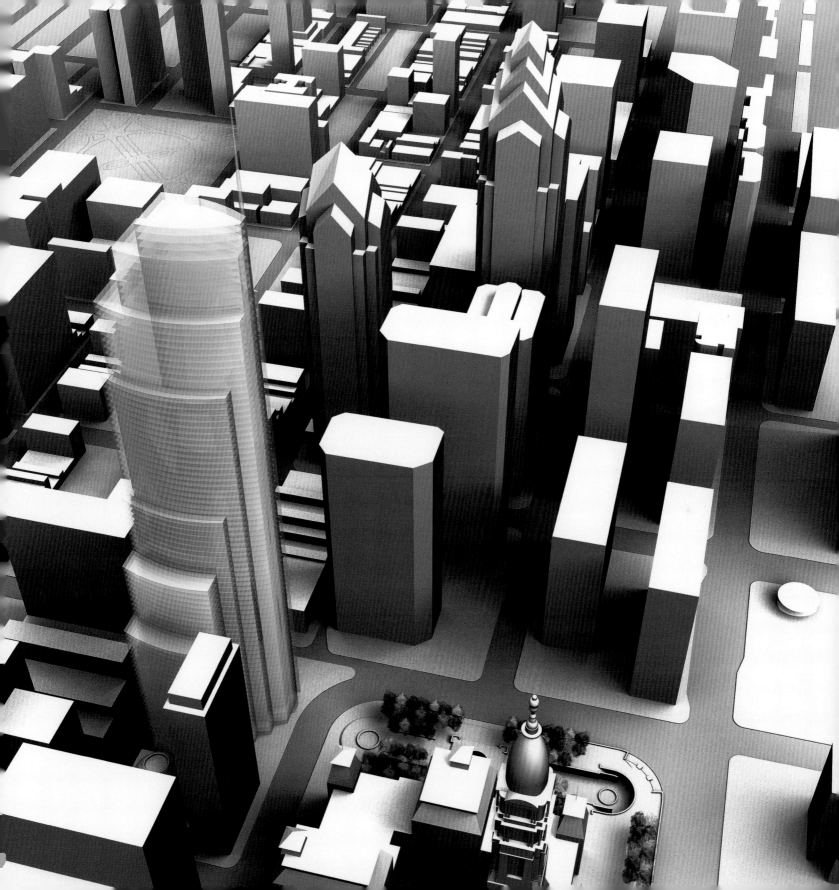

NEW ENGLAND BIOLABS COMPETITION

DESIGN: 2002
LOCATION: IPSWICH, MASSACHUSETTS
CLIENT: NEW ENGLAND BIOLABS
AREA: 150,000 SQUARE FEET (13,900 SQUARE METERS)

The New England Biolabs (NEB) headquarters facility, a world leader in the production of restriction endonucleases and other related products for molecular biology research, is a new building located in the "Great Estates" historical site in Ipswich, Massachusetts. In consideration of the founding principles of NEB, the company seeks all possible avenues to promote sound ecological practices; thus, the major design challenge was to gracefully integrate a 150,000-square-foot (13,900-square-meter) new building along with parking for 400 employees into a pristine site with restored historic buildings. The design needed to demonstrate outstanding sensitivity to its context, fully preserving its overall pastoral setting, while successfully integrating sustainable architectural principles into a modern building.

The rural setting of the 126-acre (51-hectare) site, surrounded by many additional acres of pristine conservation land, contains two major and two minor designated historic buildings. The new facility is located between the two most significant structures on the property, leaving the heart of the site open to views from both the main house and all the laboratories. The geometry of the buildings, while designed to allow the maximum amount of daylight to the winter garden and lab environment, evokes the idea of manor houses on a farm as it cascades along the crest of the hill.

Sited along the crest of the hill, the new building exterior massing is composed into four similar elements that are sympathetic to the scale of the original buildings. These four fingers are interlocked by three tropical winter gardens that serve as small oases for the scientists during the long New England winters. Purely recreational, the winter gardens contain tropical plants, birds, and butterflies. Scientists have direct access to the winter garden through the common areas and cafeteria, and operable windows from the laboratories open into these tropical spaces.

The garage is bermed and landscaped on three sides to diminish the visual impact to the northern neighbors and faced on the south with a wood lattice and metal-screen-clad walkway connecting to the laboratory buildings.

The exterior building materials are primarily a wood curtain wall and Trespa wall panel rainscreen system. The metal panel roofs will have photovoltaic panels along with skylights to the third-floor labs. The interiors are designed to be a backdrop to the client's extensive display of modern and ethnic art works and to the surrounding landscape. The overall planning creates small-scale communities that encourage collaboration within an environment expressive of investigation, art, and nature.

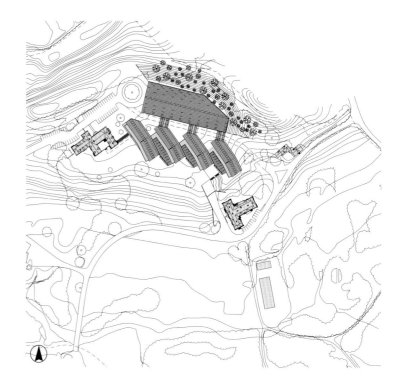

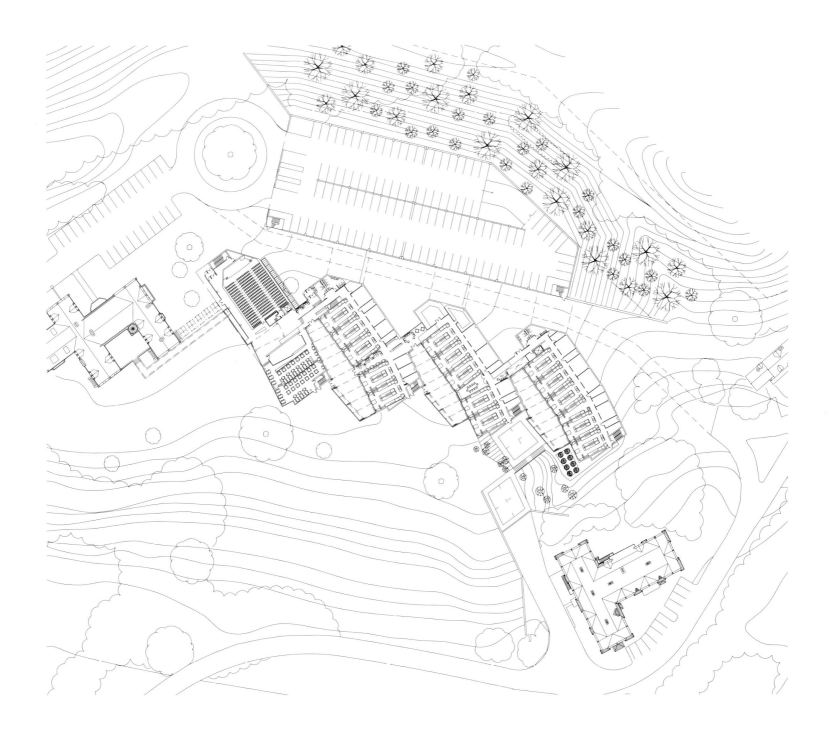

　New England Biolabs Competition

GRAND EGYPTIAN MUSEUM COMPETITION

DESIGN: 2002
LOCATION: GIZA, EGYPT
CLIENT: GRAND EGYPTIAN MUSEUM
AREA: 928,000 SQUARE FEET (86,200 SQUARE METERS)

The confluence of ancient Upper Egypt with the Nile Delta region of Lower Egypt was the fundamental historic catalyst in the formation of the Egyptian culture that produced the Grand Egyptian Museum (GEM) collection. Anchored between the metaphorical delta (Nile Park) and Upper Egypt (Dunal Park), this museum and its collection mediate cultural and intellectual forces producing the enduring Egyptian archeological legacy. The architectural proposition of the GEM, therefore, is created by erosion, infiltration, fusion of these forces, and their constituent elements—light, air, water, sand, flora, and fauna—collectively conjoined to form the physical matrix of the museum.

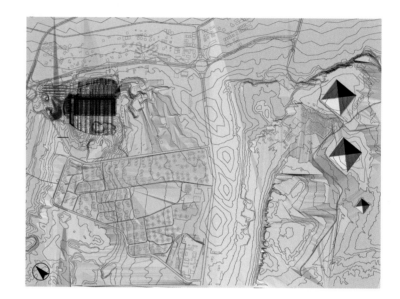

The site has been organized in zones roughly parallel to the Cairo–Alexandria Road. Vehicular access is primarily restricted to the lower elevations, with a drop-off for both buses and cars positioned directly in front of the Museum's formal entrance. The Nile Park, Theme Park, and Equipped Park form the next layer of the lower topographical area, with the extended glass façade defining an idealized edge to the higher Dunal Plateau that incorporates the natural dunes common to the western dessert.

The Museum has been placed in the middle of the site, and by means of its watercourses and paths, the activity within the walls has been extended to the various land areas beyond. With origins in the upper park, the "gift of life" canals begin their journey through the Grand Egyptian Museum, culminating in the metaphorical "delta" regions in the Nile Park. They recall the network of canals from the ancient city of Memphis that served everyday life as well as the pharaonic funerary processions to the valley temples. As visitors move from each chronological period to the next, they reference the Nile as the "source of life" throughout Egyptian history.

The symbolic message of The Grand Egyptian Museum extends beyond an archeological collection of 100,000 cultural artifacts on display in the museum proper. GEM is an interactive nodal point within the local community. The Nile Park, Theme Park, and Equipped Park are open to the greater Cairo community during and after museum hours. The Congress Hall provides meeting and lecture facilities for more than 2,500 attendees from all parts of the world. The Grand Egyptian Museum complex will reflect the Arab/Egyptian cultural values that are unique to this ancient land and a testament to the modern Egyptian culture that remains the center of the Arab world today.

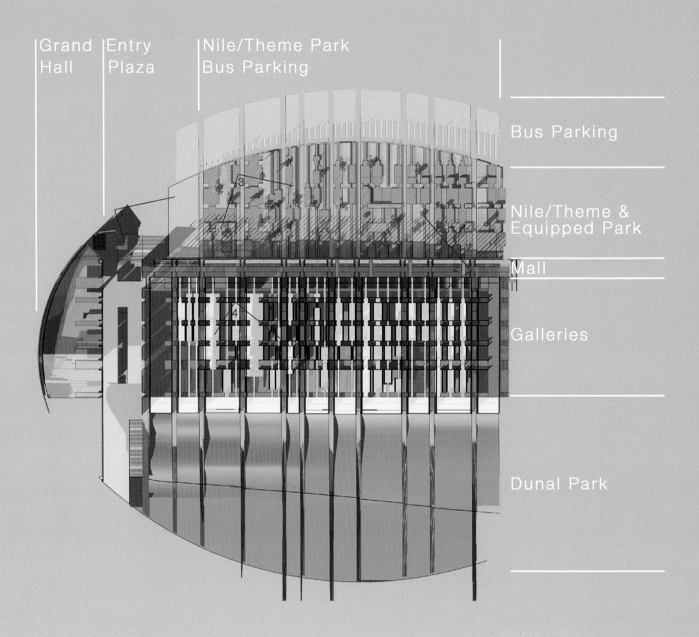

Grand
Hall

Entry
Plaza

Nile/Theme Park
Bus Parking

Bus Parking

Nile/Theme &
Equipped Park

Mall

Galleries

Dunal Park

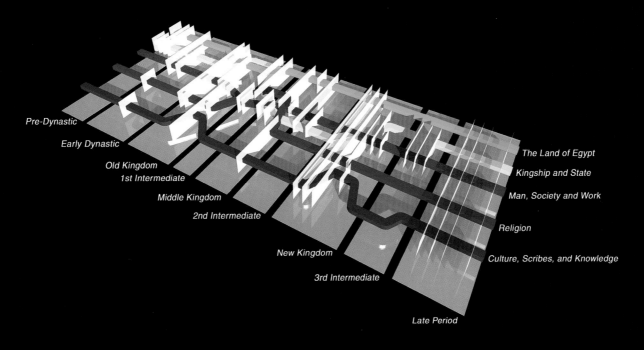

Pre-Dynastic
Early Dynastic
Old Kingdom
1st Intermediate
Middle Kingdom
2nd Intermediate
New Kingdom
3rd Intermediate
Late Period

The Land of Egypt
Kingship and State
Man, Society and Work
Religion
Culture, Scribes, and Knowledge

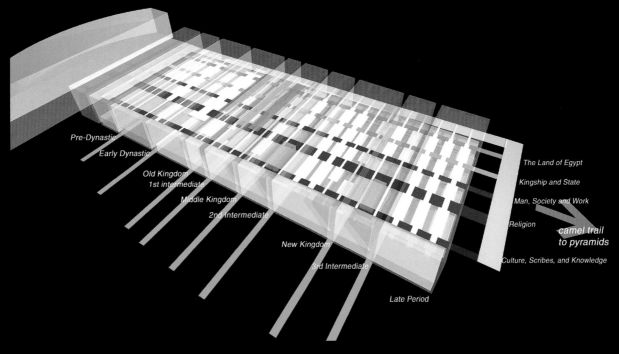

Pre-Dynastic
Early Dynastic
Old Kingdom
1st intermediate
Middle Kingdom
2nd Intermediate
New Kingdom
3rd Intermediate
Late Period

The Land of Egypt
Kingship and State
Man, Society and Work
Religion

*camel trail
to pyramids*

Culture, Scribes, and Knowledge

MONTREAL CULTURAL CENTER COMPETITION

DESIGN: 2002
LOCATION: MONTREAL, QUEBEC, CANADA
CLIENT: CITY OF MONTREAL
AREA: 900,000 SQUARE FEET (83,600 SQUARE METERS)

The democratic city is not a singular construct. Its layers of history and use, its potential as a forum for experience, and its very physical constitution and materiality are such that each citizen assembles his or her own cognitive and qualitative understanding of its identity. These readings, in turn, form a layered set of invisible cities in the hearts and minds of people that, in their sum total, comprise the true identity of Montreal.

This project presumes to operate within this urban meta-context by providing a formal, functional, and material legibility. The continuously folded plane that defines the volumes and spaces of the project is intended to operate from many points of view.

As a formal and spatial analogue, the project provides for the re-establishment of the street-wall along a majority of the site's perimeter, while directing the energy of the street up into and throughout the site, and back again out to the city. As a reconstituted public plaza, it expands the activity of the ground plane up into the upper levels of the administrative, teaching, and performance areas, and down into the subterranean network of Montreal.

As a functional device, the folded plane ties the project's constituent parts together into a cohesive whole. In contrast to a volumetric strategy of discrete buildings, it breaks down the boundaries between spaces and activities, and reconciles the tower's vertical scale with the lower elements of the project. The clearly defining regions of program function allow activities to overlap with adjacent spaces and encourage the use of the plaza for impromptu public gatherings or for planned performances, while integrating the activities on the block into the existing infrastructure.

Materially, as a glass plane, it wraps the tower to become enclosure, and releases over the courtyard to provide a tempered and sheltered semi-enclosure over the public outdoor spaces. As an opaque plane, the material recalls the texture of the site's existing industrial façades. The orientation of the tower and public plaza maximizes the amount of natural light into the open areas; the glass plane allows for entry of natural light, while the stone ground plane absorbs the sun's heat.

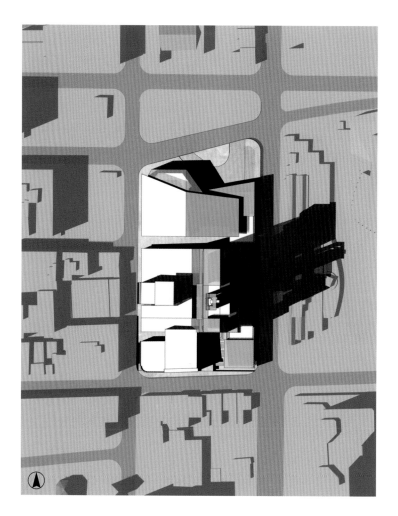

HANGZHOU INTERNATIONAL EXHIBITION AND CONFERENCE CENTER

DESIGN: 2002
LOCATION: HANGZHOU, CHINA
CLIENT: CITY OF HANGZHOU
AREA: 128,000 SQUARE FEET (11,900 SQUARE METERS)

The design intent for the exhibition/conference complex is to unify the entire facility with a graceful, undulating roof structure that recalls the graceful waters of the adjacent river and the power of the tidal bore that occasionally rushes upriver. The roof extends to embrace the low-rise portion of the 1,000-room hotel, leaving 600 rooms to rise in a round tower, recalling the historic form of the pagoda. To the south and overlooking the river, a broad staircase appears to float above a shallow water basin and also extends above the roadway, providing a walkway to the parkway along the riverbank.

The exhibition facility provides 904,000 square feet (84,000 square meters) of flexible space, distributed on three levels, each with the potential to be sub-divided into four halls that can be used independently or in combination. A 12-story office building of 215,000 square feet (20,000 square meters) overlooks the canal to the north, and a two-level retail, restaurant, and entertainment area flanks the canal promenade on both sides. Parking is provided below grade, as well as in small on-grade lots. Ramps to each of the three levels of the exhibition center allow trucks to access, unload, and load exhibits directly, and the structure has been designed to support the appropriate live loads.

Traditional wooden screens have been adapted in a modern way to provide sun protection on both the east and west façades, and a zinc roof and high-performance curtain wall anchor the design in both a historical and contemporary context. The natural beauty of the West Lake, the Qiantang River, and the Grand Canal inspired the entire design concept to further define a singular response to a very specific location.

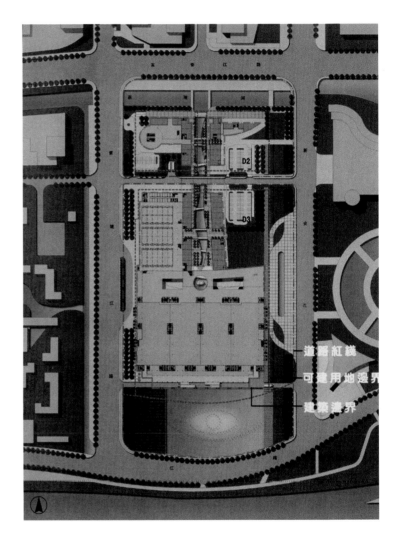

WYETH PHARMACEUTICAL HEADQUARTERS, PHASE II

DESIGN / COMPLETION: 2002 / 2003
LOCATION: COLLEGEVILLE, PENNSYLVANIA
CLIENT: WYETH PHARMACEUTICALS
AREA: 730,000 SQUARE FEET (67,800 SQUARE METERS)

The site marks the end of the Philadelphia suburbs and the beginning of open, rural hills and farms that stretch west to the Susquehanna—an area that reflects constant shifts in the light, clouds, and fields that surround it. Wyeth chose to build its headquarters here with the hope that the expansiveness and natural character would enhance its work. The company also moved to Collegeville hoping to make a place that fosters a highly energized and collaborative workforce. These two factors—Wyeth's commitment to the site and the desire to enliven its corporate culture through architecture—informed the design.

Maintaining the semi-rural character of the site and its nearly 20 acres (8 hectares) of mature forest represented a key contextual challenge. Another hurdle was relating to an existing 1,000,000-square-foot (92,900-square-meter) R&D complex that was built on the site in the late 1980s. Although Wyeth wanted its new buildings (Phase II) to be contemporary and progressive, it also wanted them to recall the existing brick structures (Phase I) with their decorative motifs and historical allusions. These concerns were addressed by using similar colors and materials and by siting the new buildings remotely along an existing radial axis. Since the new site is nearly a story higher than the original, the two complexes occupy distinct visual planes, allowing Phase II to sit obliquely from its neighbor, minimizing potential visual discrepancies.

Wyeth also chose to trade its traditional, compartmentalized office standards for a more open workplace, emphasizing public spaces filled with teaming areas, amenities, and daylight. At first, the company allowed, but then later encouraged, the development of this public realm in a bold, contemporary vocabulary and requested a prominent, corporate front door that would project the progressive aspects of the new work environment.

Phase II consists of three, four-story, 100-foot-wide (30-meter) administrative wings, clad in clear/tinted glass windows with panelized brick spandrels mounted on a structural steel frame. These wings, and the existing Phase I areas, are linked by a continuous network of two- and four-story glazed atria paved in polished Nordic Black granite. Unlike the existing Phase I that developed around an inwardly focused set of atria, all new structures frame significant landscape views. Of the 1,900 workers in Phase II, nearly all receive natural light in their workstations.

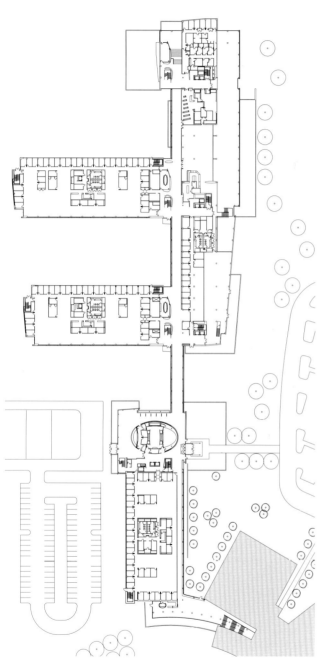

Ground floor plan

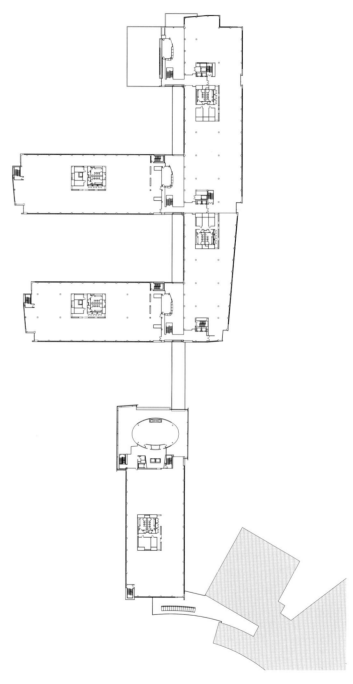

Fourth floor plan

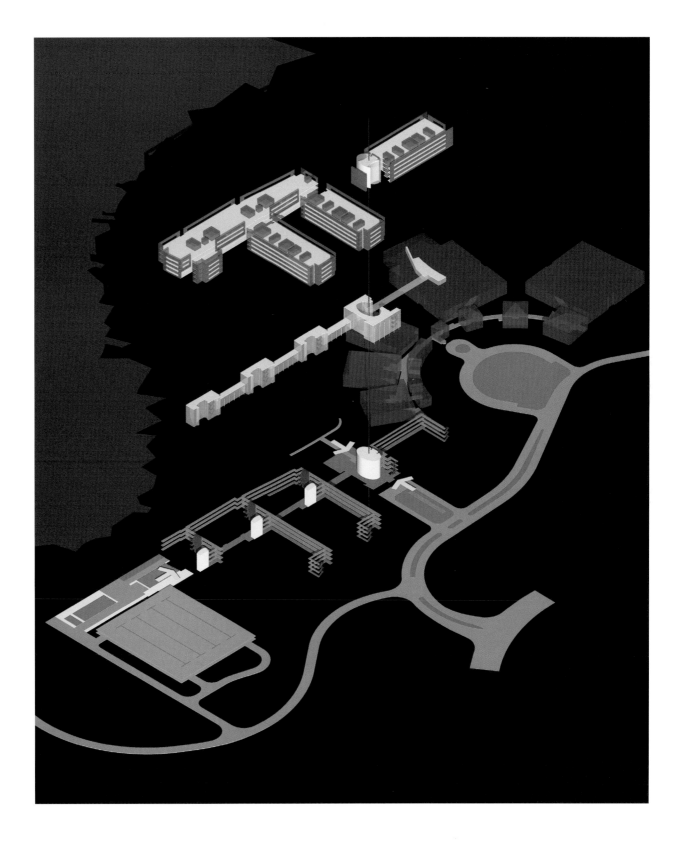

Wyeth Pharmaceutical Headquarters, Phase II

Wyeth Pharmaceutical Headquarters, Phase II

Wyeth Pharmaceutical Headquarters, Phase II

JOHNSON & JOHNSON DRUG DISCOVERY LABORATORY

DESIGN / COMPLETION: 2001 / 2004
LOCATION: LA JOLLA, CALIFORNIA
CLIENT: JOHNSON & JOHNSON PHARMACEUTICAL RESEARCH & DEVELOPMENT (J&J PRD)
AREA: 185,000 SQUARE FEET (17,200 SQUARE METERS)

The challenge was to design and construct a highly complex, 185,000-square-foot (17,200-square-meter) research facility as part of Johnson & Johnson Pharmaceutical Research & Development's La Jolla site. There had been no previous plans for expanding the site, so it was important that the new facility did not compromise either ongoing activities or the very stringent parameters of zoning and environmental concerns.

The project mission was to establish a research environment that promotes rapid discovery of potential new drugs by fostering scientific excellence and interaction within a facility that can adapt to unknown future requirements.

The realized design is a 185,000-square-foot (17,200-square-meter) addition/frontispiece to an existing structure of 122,000 square feet (11,300 square meters). The L-shaped building is organized as a laboratory block throughout the long leg and with conferencing and administrative functions contained in the perpendicular wing. Each end of the new building is tied to existing circulation patterns within the first phase facility, allowing not only ease of both pedestrian and service passage but, more importantly, facilitating interaction and enhancing the flexibility of group boundaries.

The arrival sequence begins with a new garage clad in woven stainless steel mesh and carefully buffered by perimeter planting and rooftop vine-covered trellises. A double-height lobby creates a new main entrance and leads to a new courtyard that has become the heart of the campus. The landscape design follows sustainable, low-impact practices, and local plant species are complementary to the canyon edge ecosystem.

The building's character has attempted to make a virtue out of the stringent coastal development codes by emphasizing the strong horizontality of a building absolutely limited to 30 feet (9 meters) in height. Ribbons of slightly reflective glass, horizontal aluminum mullion caps, and projecting solar shades are composed against a backdrop of Persian travertine and green serpentine. Overlapping glass planes reference the smaller-scale rhythm found on the existing building, but do so in a manner that manifests issues of daylight, the mutable nature of glass, and, again, the reinforcement of the horizontal.

Internally the building remains very much about the outside. Carefully modulated daylight pervades the public areas, the offices, and the laboratories. Views to the courtyard and to the surrounding mesas have been carefully considered in the placement and layout of the areas of congregation.

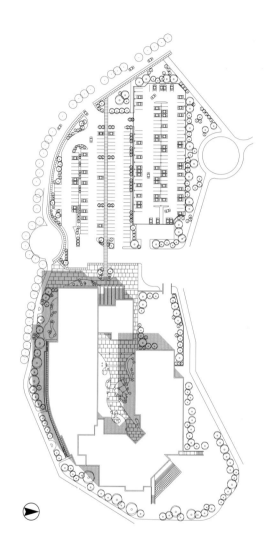

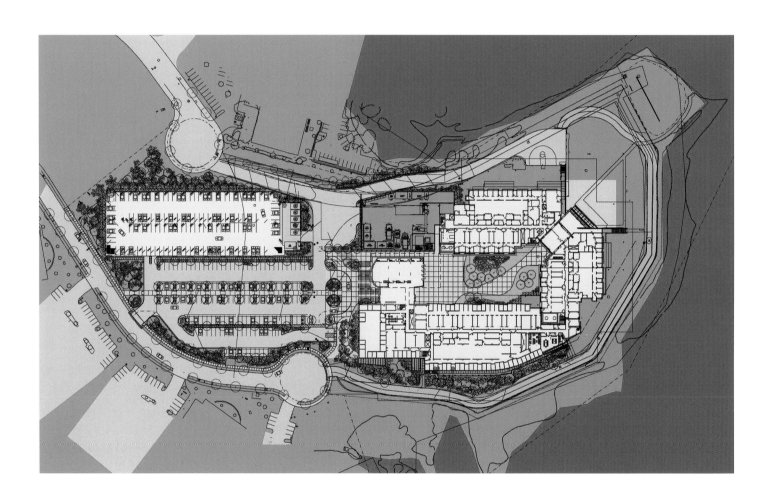

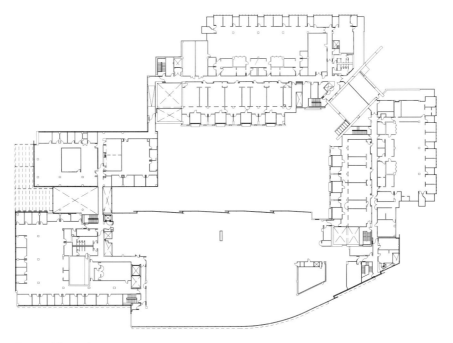

Second floor plan

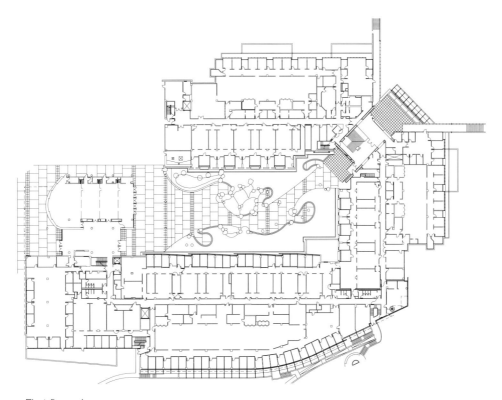

First floor plan

NBC TODAY SHOW OLYMPIC PAVILION

DESIGN / COMPLETION: 2003 / 2004
LOCATION: ATHENS, GREECE / TORINO, ITALY / BEIJING, CHINA
CLIENT: FLC MANAGEMENT
AREA: 2,800 SQUARE FEET (260 SQUARE METERS)

The primary design challenge for this project was creating modularity and transportability in a structure to be disassembled and reassembled a number of times in very different settings and environments, the first of which was the 2004 Olympic Games in Athens. The pavilion must be assembled in a matter of days at each location while minimizing site preparation. The design needed to be striking, yet simple, creating an identifiable icon for the NBC News "Today" Show and transcendent of context and style which would be inherent to the temporal personalities of each Olympic venue. The 2,800-square-foot (260-square-meter) pavilion will be used through 2012 for both summer and winter events.

The design is greatly governed by the specific technologies and flexibility required within a broadcasting studio. Inside the pavilion, an open area of approximately 1,200 square feet (110 square meters) contains three distinct sets that can be used concurrently. A "home base" set is located in the center of the studio, with an interview set and a production set on either side. Engineering and support spaces are located behind the sets. An outdoor stand-up area of 1,000 square feet (93 square meters) surrounds the pavilion, which is only elevated 3 feet (1 meter) above the ground.

The solution focused on a curved, cantilevered light steel-framed roof structure, allowing the 17-door foldaway glass storefront to establish an uninterrupted 140-degree vista of the Olympic Park. When the storefront is open, the studio space spills out onto a curved deck with a continuous stair down to grade, allowing the broadcasters to walk outside into an audience during the show. For close-up interviews inside the pavilion, a series of light-filtering panels can be moved into place. The floor system is designed with hollow planks to assist in delivering air conditioning, power, and audio/visual communications from the back of the pavilion to the studio at the front. A fabric roof stretched over a series of light steel trusses creates a distinctive profile and identity for the pavilion.

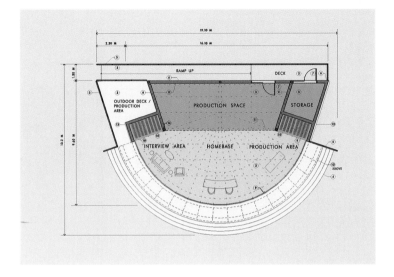

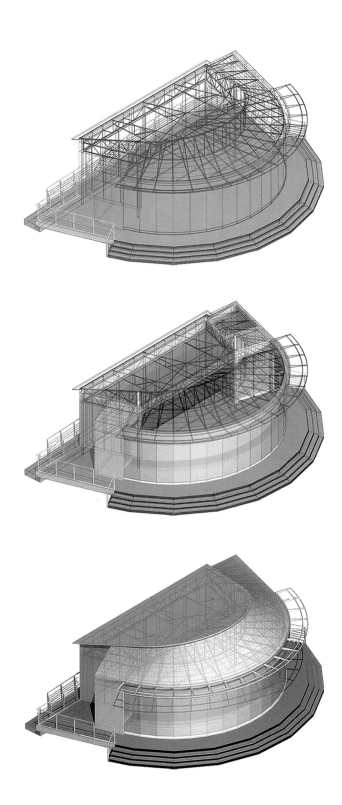

NBC Today Show Olympic Pavilion

UNIVERSITY OF PENNSYLVANIA LRSM NANOTECH CENTER

DESIGN: 2004
LOCATION: PHILADELPHIA, PENNSYLVANIA
CLIENT: UNIVERSITY OF PENNSYLVANIA
AREA: 100,500 SQUARE FEET (9,300 SQUARE METERS)

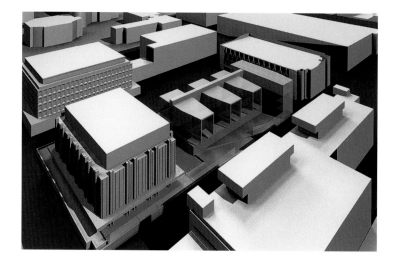

In the world of scientific academia, the research and development of nanoscience has been an active focus, especially since its application transcends any single scientific discipline. Situated near the east edge of the University of Pennsylvania's campus and conjoined with the Laboratory for Research on the Structure of Matter (LRSM), the Nanotechnology Center for the School of Engineering is sited in a location challenged by existing constraints, but with the inherent opportunity to present the university's ongoing commitment to research. As a basis of design, the new scheme addresses three different scales and constituents: the campus; the identity of the School of Engineering; and the individual participants involved in teaching, learning, and discovery, for whom the new facility will be critical to their respective successes.

The new LRSM is envisioned as a connector, tying various academic groups together and creating an intimate courtyard as a center for the scientific community. Massed as a series of semi-discrete elements tied together by a large cantilevered glass awning, the building is sympathetic to the physical characteristics of the surrounding campus structures. Clad in curtain wall framed by brick, the new building provides evidence of the research activities within, while being architecturally expressive of the technological focus of these endeavors.

The project program includes nano-fabrications, micro-fabrications, electron microscopy, and particle accelerator laboratories. Support areas include faculty and investigator offices, classrooms, a library, and an auditorium. Public outreach educational facilities help integrate the new building within a broader city context.

MITRE CENTER

DESIGN / COMPLETION: 2003 / 2004
LOCATION: BEDFORD, MASSACHUSETTS
CLIENT: MITRE CORPORATION
AREA: 96,000 SQUARE FEET (8,900 SQUARE METERS)

MITRE Corporation, a not-for-profit research and development organization specializing in systems engineering, information technology, operational concepts, and enterprise modernization, creates technologies used by the Department of Defense, the Federal Aviation Administration, the Internal Revenue Service, and the Treasury Department. The design task was to reconfigure the campus to bring all major circulation routes into a town square and to design a new central facility around that square that fosters collaboration in both formal and spontaneous settings.

The new MITRE Center is the high-profile gateway building to MITRE Corporation's 100-acre (40-hectare) Bedford campus. A three-story building of approximately 96,000 square feet (8,900 square meters), the MITRE Center includes a central campus cafeteria with seating for 400, a large conference center, demonstration classrooms on the first two floors, and executive and general office areas on the third floor. Special features of the building include technology demonstration rooms such as the "Immersion" room where large, high-definition monitors display flight simulation programs and similar tools.

Together the new campus plan and the new building transform MITRE's working environment. The campus entry is accorded a dignity commensurate with MITRE's work; and a vast new array of enhanced common functions are centrally available to both employees and clients.

Numerous environmentally sensitive features were included in the project: a 1,700-square-foot (160-square-meter) array of solar panels is deployed on the roof, generating 16,900 kilowatt-hours of electricity annually; a solar entrance canopy supplements this production with another 12,500 kilowatt-hours; high-efficiency plumbing fixtures are used to reduce water consumption by 30 percent; high-performance glazing, increased insulation, sun-shading devices, daylight harvesting and high-efficiency mechanical systems are used to reduce energy consumption by 35 percent; 90 percent of construction and demolition waste were diverted from landfill disposal; indoor air quality is enhanced with the construction IAQ program, CO_2 monitoring, low-emitting paints, carpets, adhesives and sealants and a Green housekeeping program.

As a way of educating staff and visitors to this initiative, an interactive educational panel has been located on the second floor, displaying a vast array of information, including the amount of electricity being generated by the solar cells. The project received the LEED® Silver Certification status from the US Green Building Council.

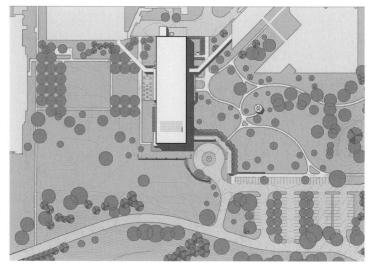

AQUARIUM COMPETITION

DESIGN: 2004
LOCATION: SUZHOU, CHINA
CLIENT: CITY OF SUZHOU
AREA: 227,000 SQUARE FEET (21,000 SQUARE METERS)

An aquarium encapsulates a broad world into an environment that creates precious relationships between man and creature, land and sea, history and evolution. It is a place that we understand as an extension of the rivers, seas, and oceans that constitute both the world we know, and a much larger reality that we usually can only read or dream about. It is a building that not only allows, but necessitates, discovery.

The design for the Suzhou Aquarium owes much to metaphor and association. From fish, we borrowed the characteristics of grace of movement, translucency and iridescence, and especially, awe. From water, the qualities of ebb and flow, transparency and reflectivity, and, above all else, mystery, were appropriated. Fluidity was the premise of the design.

The aquarium had a complex program of public function and main exhibit areas. A 10,800-square-foot (1,000-square-meter) entrance hall with proximity to the Auditorium and IMAX Theater begins the three-dimensional circulation route. Walkways, ramps, and tunnels lead from coastline pools to deep ocean exhibits, from tropical fish environments to Pacific Ocean tanks—providing passage beside, beneath, and within the fish lairs. A marine library bridges the realm between the public venues and the more private administration offices, research laboratories, and extensive support areas.

Beyond its critical relationship to the reality of an aquarium, water has also been integral to the traditions of Suzhou's gardens and canals, so it is appropriate that its ever-changing presence has influenced the building enclosure. Glass and metal with various degrees of reflectivity enter into a never-ending dialogue with both the surface of the lake and the sky, as if the building were not really an imposition of man.

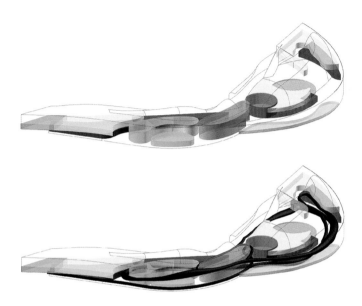

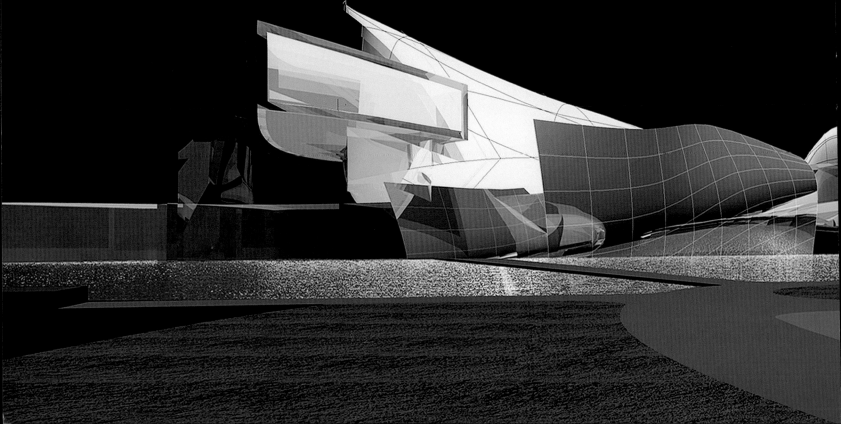

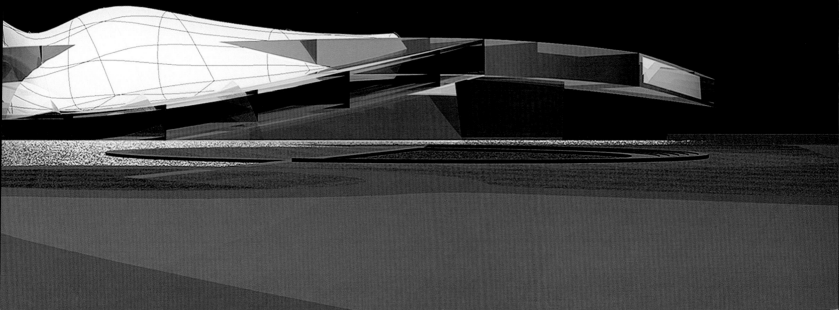

UNIVERSITY OF COLORADO HEALTH SCIENCES CENTER, RC1

(IN ASSOCIATION WITH FENTRESS ARCHITECTS)

DESIGN / COMPLETION: 2001 / 2004
LOCATION: AURORA, COLORADO
CLIENT: UNIVERSITY OF COLORADO AT DENVER AND HEALTH SCIENCES CENTER
AREA: 622,000 SQUARE FEET (57,800 SQUARE METERS)

Research Complex 1 of the University of Colorado Health Sciences Center is designed as two freestanding buildings of eight and eleven stories, linked by pedestrian bridges at several levels. The entire facility encompasses 462,000 square feet (42,900 square meters) of wet research laboratory, 92,000 square feet (8,500 square meters) of office and conference areas, 46,000 square feet (4,300 square meters) of vivarium facilities, and 22,000 square feet (2,000 square meters) of an educational component. The southernmost building, the tallest, defines the threshold of the research quadrangle and houses departments whose proximity to the clinical building to the south is critical. The north building houses several interrelated components: the educational component on the first floor level, which brings a hub of activity at the edge of the main campus walkway and on the courtyard, and those departments on the upper floor that require a larger floor plate than the south building offered.

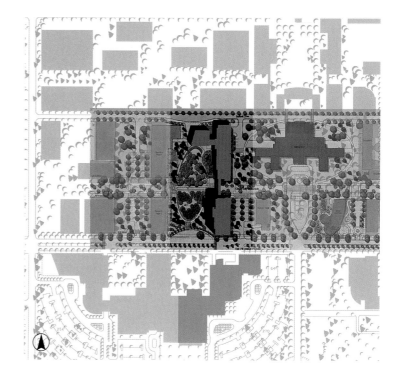

The most critical component for both buildings is the second floor where the double-height walkway, located on the courtyard side, is perceived to be suspended on air and becomes the great connector. The walkway culminates at the first and second floors at the auditorium/conference wing, which contains a 200- and 100-seat teaching auditorium as well a large conference room. In order to encourage discovery and innovation in a multi-disciplinary environment, the location of the enclosed faculty member offices became the critical component of the plans. The design uses a public corridor as the generator of interaction and as a distinct circulation component of each floor. Departmental suites flank the ends of the corridors. A separate linear equipment corridor not only serves as the access for the labs and service elevators, but also houses the lab equipment, thus reducing the noise level of the laboratories.

The three principal materials on the building's exterior are brick, metal, and curtain wall. The brick becomes the envelope for the laboratories, the metal is used for the support and equipment storage, and the glass dresses the offices and public spaces. The massing and materiality of the building materials evolve from the solidity of the brick to the transparency and elusiveness of the glass, a transformation meant to evoke the scientific process of discovery.

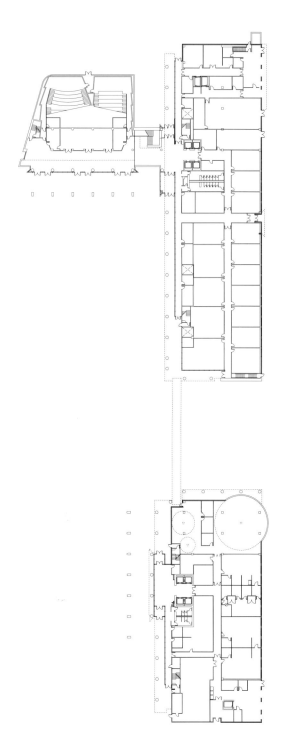

First floor plan

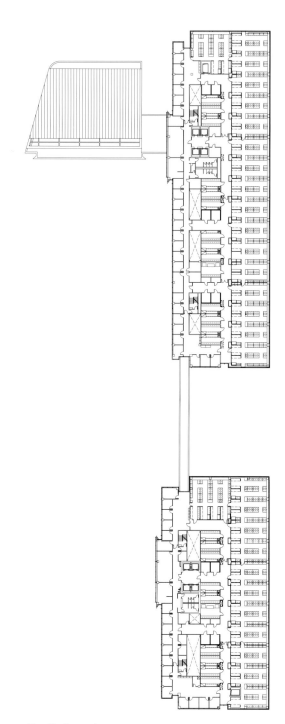

Fourth floor plan

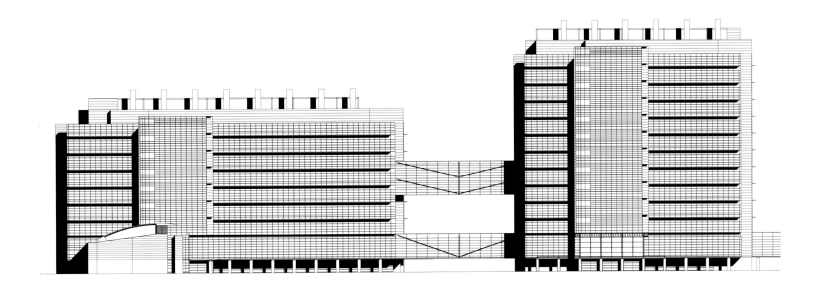

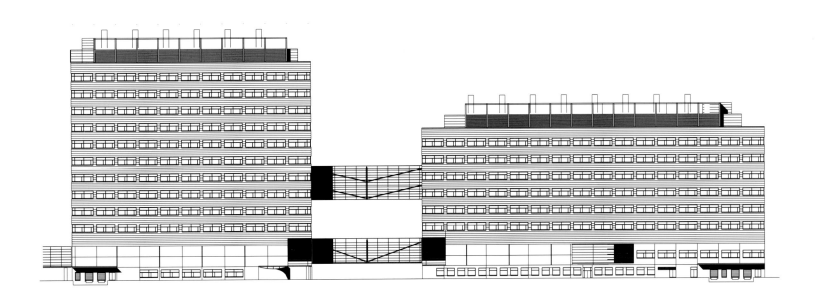

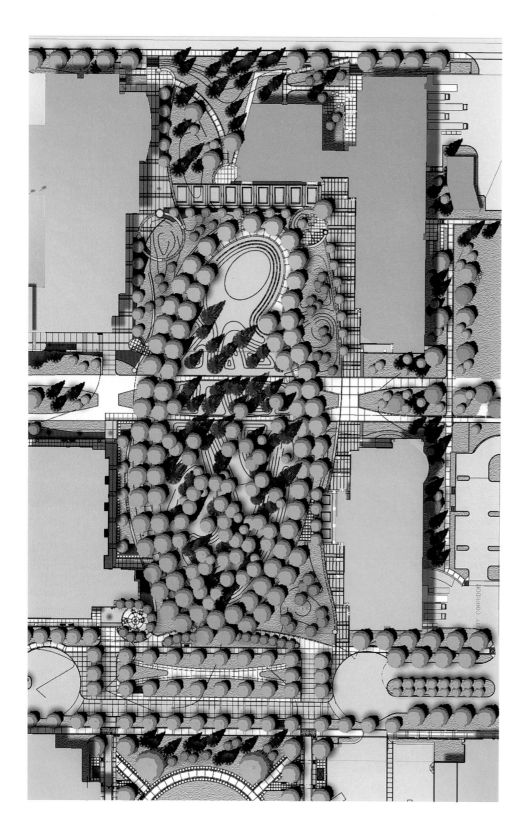

University of Colorado Health Sciences Center, RC1

University of Colorado Health Sciences Center, RC1

NOVARTIS WORLD HEADQUARTERS

DESIGN / COMPLETION: 2002 / 2004
LOCATION: CAMBRIDGE, MASSACHUSETTS
CLIENT: NOVARTIS INSTITUTES FOR BIOMEDICAL RESEARCH
AREA: 500,000 SQUARE FEET (46,500 SQUARE METERS)

When Novartis, one of the world's leading biotechnology companies, made the strategic decision to establish its worldwide research headquarters in Cambridge, Massachusetts, it was evident that it could not be an ordinary project. One of the key drivers was to create an environment that would greatly enhance collaboration among the staff as well as accelerate the overall pace of drug discovery, which can easily take a decade or more and cost a billion dollars. Novartis sought to create a technically refined facility that could support today's technology as well as respond to the demands of ever-evolving areas of research.

The chosen site was the historic NECCO building on Massachusetts Avenue in Cambridge. When originally built in 1923, it was the largest building in the world that was solely devoted to the manufacture of candy. Converting this industrial building into high-tech research labs required both a leap of imagination and close attention to the technical details. The key design gesture was to cut a six-story amoeba-shaped atrium at the center of the H-shaped plan. Into this open, airy, and skylit space were inserted four specially designed and engineered glass elevators— perfectly cylindrical and perfectly transparent. Embedded in the floor pattern of the main lobby is a large strand of DNA that symbolizes the mission and purpose of the building to all who enter it.

From this main space, primary circulation spines lead directly to the laboratory areas. Transparent circular conference areas, or "bubble rooms," were placed at the intersection of key corridors. The laboratory wings are arranged in parallel layers: corridors, open office areas, and then the laboratories themselves. There are direct views from the corridors through the offices to the labs, reinforcing the sense of lightness and transparency throughout the building. The major lab spaces, some of which are 300 feet (90 meters) in length, are supported by overhead service carriers and mobile casework so that they can be rearranged quickly as research teams set and then reconfigure their equipment. As part of the project, the existing boiler plant was converted to a new cafeteria and conference center, connected by a landscaped exterior courtyard to the main building.

The 500,000-square-foot (46,500-square-meter) Novartis project earned "Lab of the Year" honors for its innovation in lab design and technology as well as a *Business Week/Architectural Record* award for design excellence that directly contributed to the enhancement of Novartis' strategic mission.

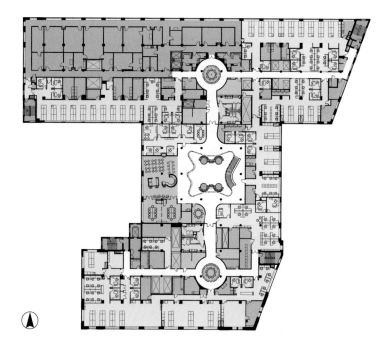

MERCK RESEARCH LABORATORIES (MRL) BOSTON

DESIGN / COMPLETION: 2000 / 2004
LOCATION: BOSTON, MASSACHUSETTS
CLIENT: MERCK & CO., INC.
AREA: 615,000 SQUARE FEET (57,100 SQUARE METERS)

The design of the Merck Research Laboratories Boston (MRL Boston) was governed by a set of goals and aspirations that shared in the creation of an environment that not only supports, but contributes to, the practice of scientific research.

MRL Boston is a 615,000-square-foot (57,100-square-meter), 12-story research laboratory tower with six levels of below-grade parking that is located in the Longwood Medical Area of Boston, a highly active educational, cultural, and historical environment. The site is at the juncture of high-rise institutional buildings to the west and south, and the lower-scaled academic buildings to the east and north. As a result of the building's adjacencies, considerations of scale, material, function, and site geometry were paramount in the design process. Given the context within which MRL Boston exists, a sympathetic, not similar, response seemed appropriate. To achieve a singular identity, the materials and coloration chosen, while not identified with the surrounding institutions, were instead coupled with many other aspects of design to allow the building to present itself uniquely.

Massing is a direct reaction to the dimensional site limitations along with the very different context on each of the four sides. The laboratory tower is similar in scale to the research and healthcare facilities to the south, and the northern extension corresponds to the maximum height within Emmanuel College. The juncture between the two components is given definition by an atrium that is at the terminus of the entry drive. Here, the various geometries of the site converge to define the atrium space—a space that serves as a collector of people and events on the ground floor and as an artery that binds the tower to its lower wing with bridges on the second, third, and fourth floors.

The program's resolution has been the obvious point of departure; and, although there existed many dictates respective to adjacency and interrelationship, the design has been further influenced by concerns for flexibility and adaptability. The building is divided programmatically between the tower and the low wing. The complex program consists of chemistry, biology, and pharmacology laboratories with all the attendant support spaces, as well as offices, conferencing and interaction areas, cafeteria, auditorium, and library. The private functions of research are housed within the tower with restrictions of access depending on the level of security required. The open and shared spaces as well as administrative offices are located in the low wing and are less restrictive in terms of access. Plan determinations have been made with consideration for movement from public to private, between laboratories, support and office areas, and along routes that promote interaction.

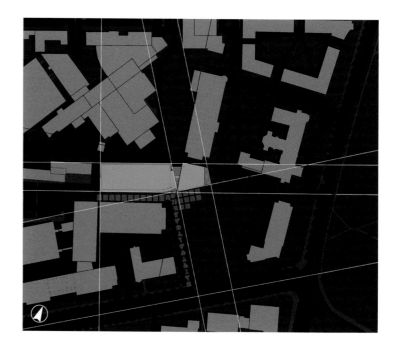

Throughout the facility, the provision of daylight has been a fundamental driver. The building is encased entirely in glass, a departure from the predominant context of red brick, beige brick, and precast concrete. The west wall reflects the more introspective nature of research with its strip windows and a larger spandrel condition. The east wall along which the offices are located consists of a combination of clear vision glass and a shadow box spandrel condition of silk-screened glass with a reflective back up panel. A sloping 12-foot-high (4-meter) ceiling and clerestory window allow significant light into the interior offices and corridor. The planarity of the skin is further emphasized by the multiple layerings of the glass wall as it sweeps gently by the atrium and the low wing. The varying programmatic functions behind the glass are subtly revealed by the glass wall as it undergoes its transformation from one type of space to another.

The character of the building was influenced by issues of program and adjacencies, but more directly by deliberate decisions involving imagery, and on the existing and planned conditions of its immediate and city-wide context. The design is very much about the interface with light; no other consideration is seen as so contributory to ultimately providing a range of experiences. The building's enclosure, while satisfying criteria of comfort, containment, and security, is more about the many presentation possibilities than it is about boundary. The architectural character endeavors to be understood in terms that are readily associated with scientific research, technology, and discovery, affording both the viewers of the building and the participants within layers of experience.

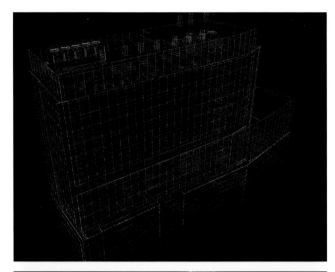

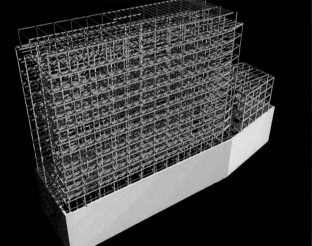

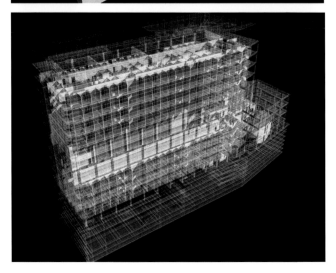

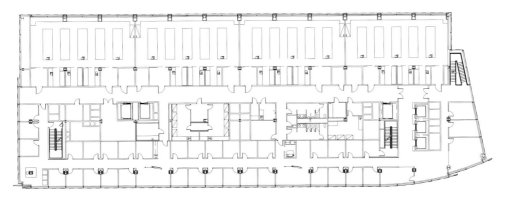

Eighth floor plan

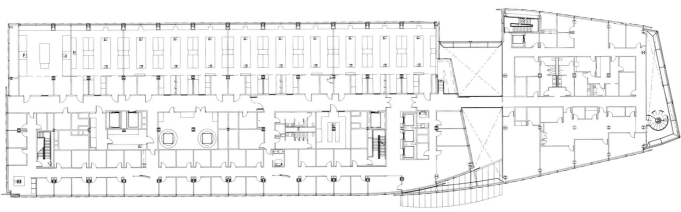

Second floor plan

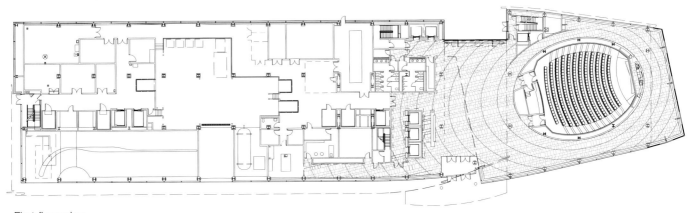

First floor plan

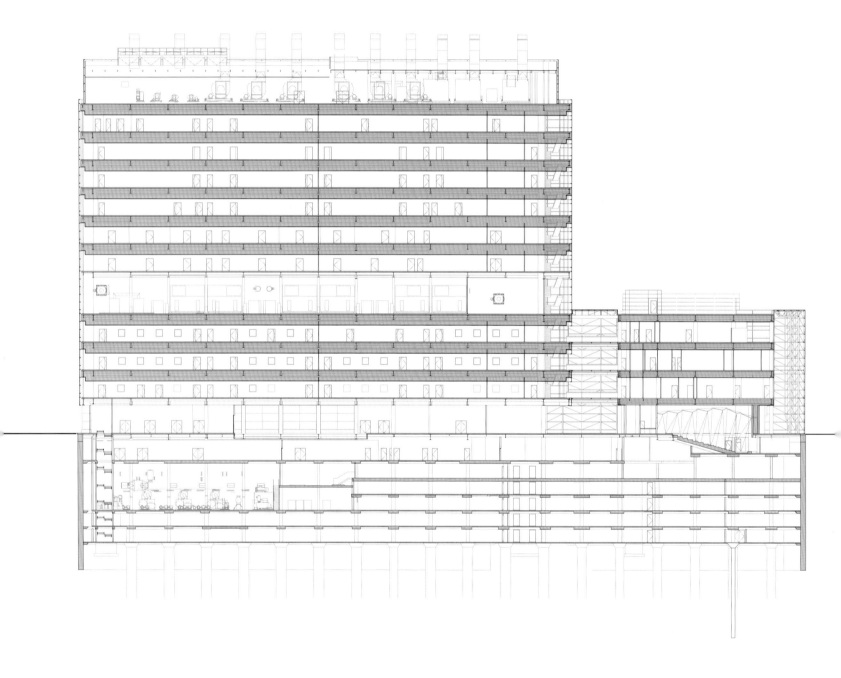

214   Merck Research Laboratories Boston

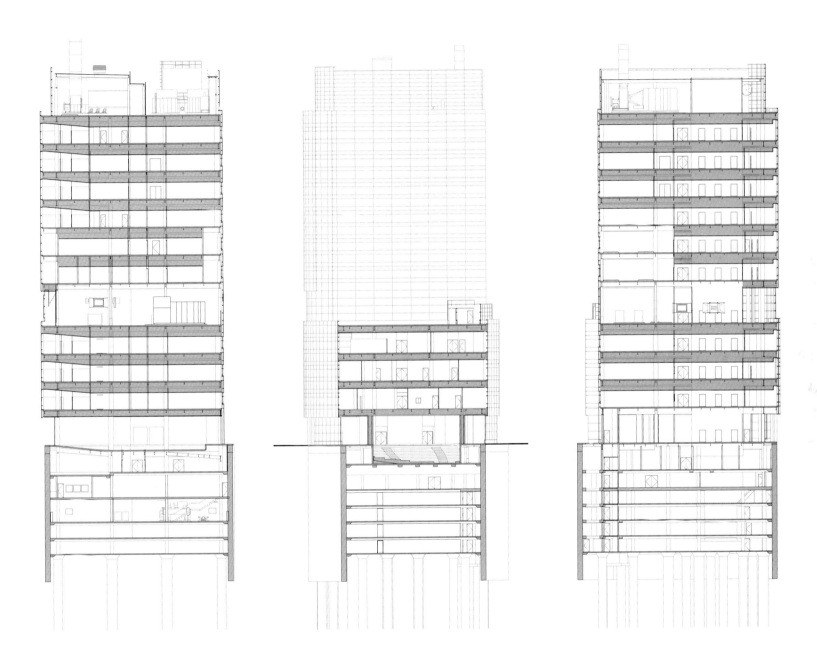

Merck Research Laboratories Boston

Merck Research Laboratories Boston

Merck Research Laboratories Boston

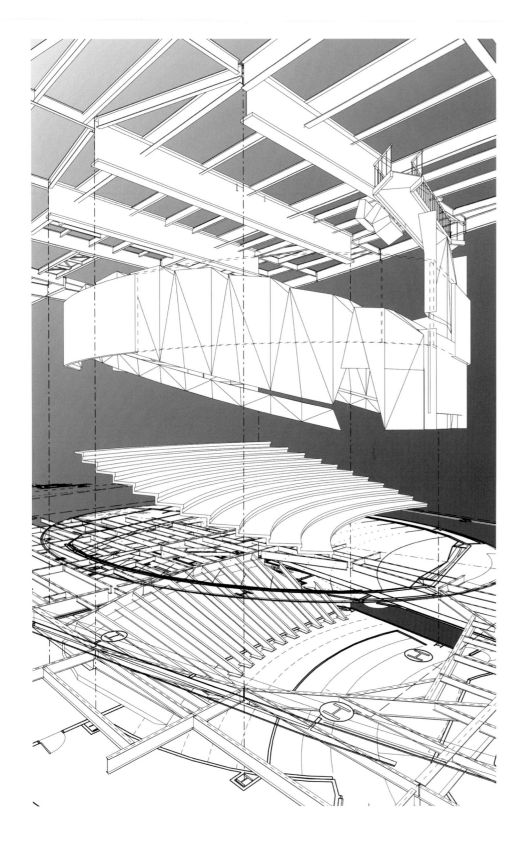

Zhiye Plaza Office Tower
Suzhou, China

Avery Dennison Headquarters
Mentor, Ohio

SAP Competition
Newtown Square, Pennsylvania

The News & Observer Downtown Office Tower
Raleigh, North Carolina

University of Colorado Health Sciences Center, RC2
Aurora, Colorado

ACE INA Corporate Headquarters
Philadelphia, Pennsylvania

Rockefeller University Comparative Bioscience Center Annex
New York, New York

Wyeth Chemical Development Laboratory Addition
Pearl River, New York

Lincoln University New Science/High Technology Building
Chester County, Pennsylvania

University of Delaware Brown Chemistry Lab Renovation
Newark Delaware

Amgen Helix Campus Expansion Plan
Seattle, Washington

CIGNA Corporate Headquarters Renovation
Philadelphia, Pennsylvania

DEA Clandestine Lab
Quantico, Virginia

Emerson College Piano Row Residence Hall
Boston, Massachusetts

MedImmune, Inc. Administrative & Training Facility
Gaithersburg, Maryland

Pfizer Worldwide Safety Sciences Toxicology Center
Ann Arbor, Michigan

EFFECT

05

EFFECT

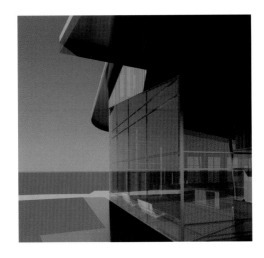  

322 "A" STREET OFFICE AND MANUFACTURING BUILDING

DESIGN / COMPLETION: 2004 / 2005
LOCATION: WILMINGTON, DELAWARE
CLIENT: THE BUCCINI/POLLIN GROUP AND E.J. DESETA
AREA: 94,000 SQUARE FEET (8,700 SQUARE METERS)

Located in Wilmington, Delaware, this office and manufacturing building is as much a story about an individual as it is about a building. The client was required, 40 years ago, to leave Art College and help her mother run the family sheet metal business after the death of her father. She stepped into the leadership position and made the business prosperous while raising a family and later helped her sons start a very successful real estate development company. To this day, the company continues as a sheet metal and ornamental metal business, and its new building houses both offices and the metal fabrication shop. In the tradition of keeping the family together, a portion of the building is also home to the owner's sons' real estate development company.

The client wanted a facility that would highlight her company's trade and craft. The architecture of the building explored the use of metal not only as the building skin and mechanical distribution network, but also took advantage of the company production capabilities to fabricate custom-designed building partitions, casework, and furniture.

The 94,000-square-foot (8,700-square-meter) building is clearly split to reflect the two parts of the program: a single-story metal fabrication workshop (70,000 square feet/6,500 square meters) and two levels of office area (24,000 square feet/2,200 square meters). The office building is elevated to create a covered parking area underneath, raise the occupied spaces above the 100-year flood plain, and assure that the presence at the street intersection is given due prominence. The lower-level offices house the metal fabrication administration and connect through a bridge to a mezzanine in the shop. The third level is the headquarters of the real estate development company. The building is book-ended by two high spaces: a three-story lobby atrium that functions as exhibition space for company products and a double-height common space oriented toward the river and the city.

The material palette consists of two primary materials: zinc flat-lock panels manufactured and installed by the client are used to highlight people spaces, and pre-manufactured, field-assembled corrugated metal panels are used for the workshop. Glass curtain wall assemblies present the multi-story gathering areas to the public and provide near and distant views to the occupants.

The office floor plan is only 60 feet (18 meters) wide. Offices, located on the perimeter, and all conference rooms are enclosed by client-made translucent shoji screens or transparent glass walls fabricated with painted steel angles and exposed fasteners. The desks, tables, and credenzas within were all produced by the client's shop and continue the integration of design and manufacturing to showcase metalwork as a craft.

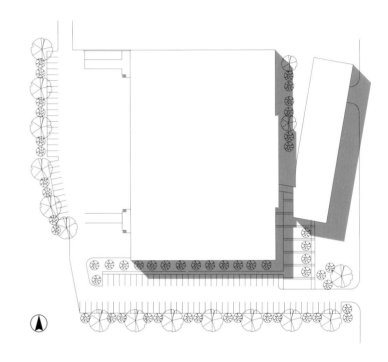

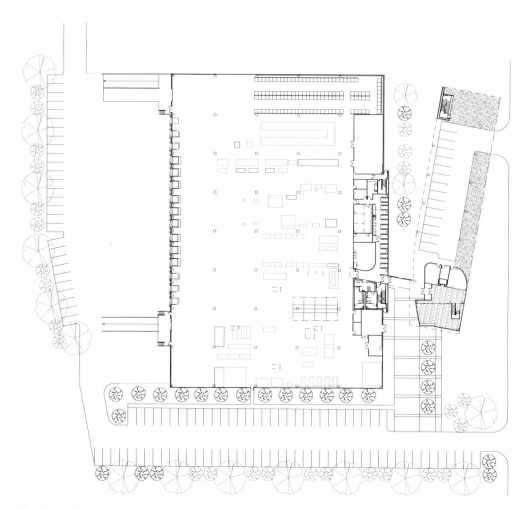

First floor plan

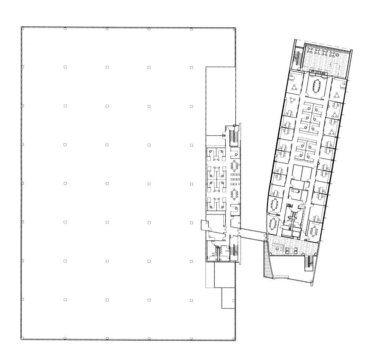

Second floor plan

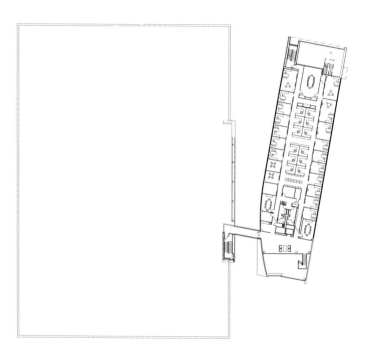

Third floor plan

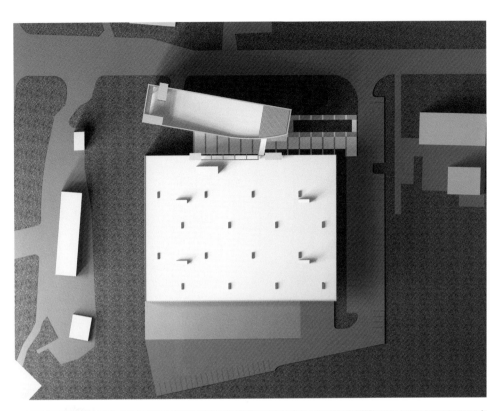

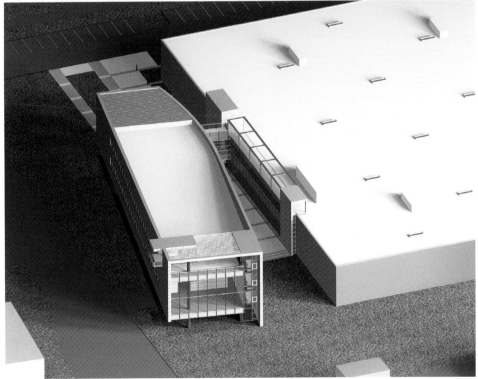

322 "A" Street Office and Manufacturing Building

322 "A" Street Office and Manufacturing Building

322 "A" Street Office and Manufacturing Building

322 "A" Street Office and Manufacturing Building

BD TECHNOLOGIES DATA CENTER AND OFFICE EXPANSION

DESIGN / COMPLETION: 2004 / 2005
LOCATION: RESEARCH TRIANGLE PARK, NORTH CAROLINA
CLIENT: BD TECHNOLOGIES
AREA: 16,000 SQUARE FEET (1,490 SQUARE METERS)

BD Technologies constructed a 16,000-square-foot (1,490-square-meter), two-story expansion of its existing data center facilities in Research Triangle Park. The exterior design is intended to complement the architectural character of the existing building, employing the same palette of materials and colors of the original building, with ribbed metal siding and red painted metal accents, cast-in-place concrete, and dark brown aluminum sash with aluminum sun shades on the south and west façades.

The simple, rectangular shape of the addition creates a very flexible open office space on the second floor and maintains the straightforward character of the original building. In contrast, the UPS/battery room is articulated as an architecturally distinct, one-story curving element that is integrated into the landscape and serves to screen the large generators and other grade-mounted equipment from view from the main entrance, and creates a foil for the extensive landscaping on the site.

The interior design supports BD Technologies' stated goal of creating an open work environment that fosters "communication and sharing." The light-filled, loft-like second-floor space will allow for maximum flexibility in the layout of workstations, with meeting rooms and group work and break areas that support more specialized activities.

All interior partitions are non-structural, allowing for maximum flexibility in reconfiguring interior layouts. A long-span structural bay accommodates a large, column-free data center with further expansion potential. Stairs, elevators, and other fixed elements are located at the building perimeter to maximize future flexibility.

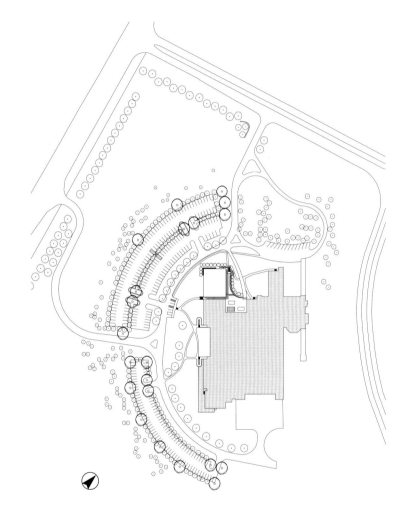

UNITED STATES POSTAL SERVICE PROCESSING AND DISTRIBUTION CENTER

DESIGN / COMPLETION: 2003 / 2005
LOCATION: PHILADELPHIA, PENNSYLVANIA
CLIENT: UNITED STATES POSTAL SERVICE
AREA: 930,000 SQUARE FEET (86,400 SQUARE METERS)

High technology is changing the United States Postal Service (USPS). The next generation of mail processing called for the design of this 930,000-square-foot (86,400-square-meter) prototypical project for Philadelphia that will act as a model for planned facilities across the country. The USPS Processing and Distribution Center moved all activities from its Center City location on 30th Street to a new location in South Philadelphia in close proximity to I-95 and the Philadelphia International Airport, thereby implementing a more efficient means of distribution.

The Postal Service has enhanced and improved its capabilities with an advanced computer-aided network that processes mail with greater accuracy than ever before. This sophisticated operation extends over an expansive two-level workroom totaling 630,000 square feet (58,500 square meters) that extensively utilizes mechanized equipment and conveying systems. Shipping/receiving, support, and mechanical areas surround both levels of the processing function.

A three-story-high circulation spine links the work and administrative areas while concentrating and securely organizing employee movement through the facility. Infused with light during the day and dramatically lit at night, this environment has been designed to welcome the employees and provide a respite from the highly functional workroom.

The architectural expression of the building is derived from the character of the tripartite program of shipping, processing, and administration, and the restrictive site conditions. Three sides are devoted to the realities of truck traffic. The center is a clear representation of the enormous volume of the processing area and the myriad required mechanical and life safety support elements. The administrative component, in negotiating the interface with the adjacent neighborhood and in presenting the image of USPS to the city as a whole, is more humanly scaled and more preciously clad.

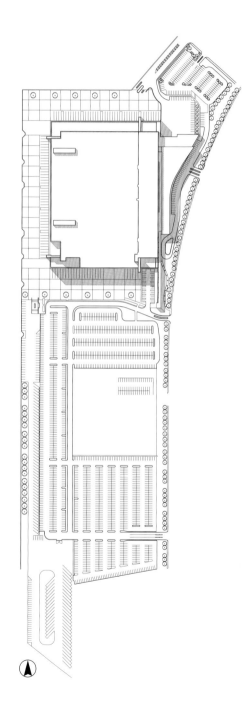

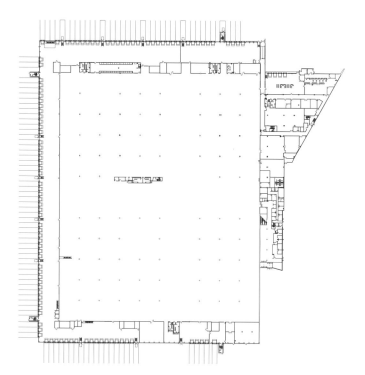

First floor plan

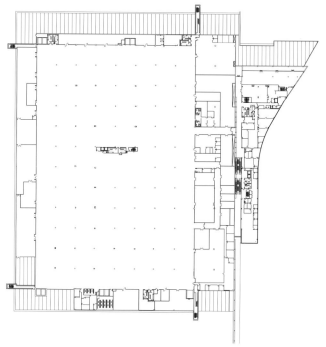

Third floor plan

SCIENCE CENTER TECHNOLOGY PARK MASTER PLAN

DESIGN: 2005
LOCATION: PHILADELPHIA, PENNSYLVANIA
CLIENT: SCIENCE CENTER
AREA: 2,000,000 SQUARE FEET (186,000 SQUARE METERS)

For years, West Philadelphia has shown tremendous promise to become a world-class academic and business incubator on par with Cambridge and San Francisco. Several nationally recognized institutions in the area, including the University of Pennsylvania, Drexel University, the Hospital at the University of Pennsylvania Health System, and the Children's Hospital of Philadelphia, are highly competitive at drawing the kind of researchers, knowledge workers, and graduate students who support these other entrepreneurial models. However, in recent years, there has been a noticeable lag in the quantity and quality of West Philadelphia's research infrastructure—particularly in the biosciences. The Science Center aims to be the physical and intellectual catalyst of the area's transformation from a "good to great" hub for this kind of research and commercialization.

Currently, the Science Center is engaged in an ambitious plan to add between 1,000,000 and 2,000,000 square feeet (92,900 and 186,000 square meters) of mixed-use, research-intensive space to its properties along Market Street. At the core of the plan is the goal to add nearly 1,000,000 square feet (92,900 square meters) of research space by the year 2015. Given contemporary trends in knowledge communities, the new Science Center plan is committed to a mixed-use program that includes sizable areas for work, life, and entertainment. Current plans will add approximately 400 units of housing, 250 units of accommodation, and nearly 100,000 square feet (9,300 square meters) of retail and medical office to the existing campus. Most of these new retail and office spaces will form a continuous street edge along Market Street, animating and increasing the sense of a vibrant, pedestrian enclave.

Conceptually, the plan aims to create a more open "metropolitan" feel to the Science Center. Rather than making all the buildings similar in scale and material, the new plan will encourage buildings that vary in scale and material—some large, some small—more in keeping with a typical city street and less like an isolated campus. The plan will also use ground-level retail to turn corners and encourage cross traffic along 34th, 36th, and 38th Streets, encouraging casual interactions with the surrounding neighborhoods and institutions, expanding and anchoring West Philadelphia as a true "Knowledge Community."

WILMINGTON INTERMODAL TRANSIT CENTER

DESIGN: 2005
LOCATION: WILMINGTON, DELAWARE
CLIENT: DELAWARE DEPARTMENT OF TRANSPORTATION
AREA: 45,000 SQUARE FEET (4,200 SQUARE METERS)

This design calls for a full-block, 600-car parking structure with accommodation for bus traffic (Delaware Area Rapid Transit and Greyhound) within the structure on the site's western edge and along adjacent Walnut Street. Beyond fulfilling all programmatic and operational requirements, the Transit Center is designed to enhance its immediate urban site, to reinforce the location's pivotal role in linking downtown to the riverfront, and to join with the Frank Furness-designed train station in welcoming visitors to the city.

Along Walnut Street, the shared bus station and the public functions of DelDOT (information, ticketing and sales, and community outreach programs) activate the pedestrian environment. The upper three stories contain the office requirements of the Department of Transportation in an open and highly flexible space where daylight is the primary attribute. A linear bar of building support spaces separates the office space from the garage to the east.

The ground floor of the garage has been carefully planned in response to the arrival and departure requirements of the interstate bus traffic and both the movement and short-term parking of the intrastate vehicles. Parking access and egress is separated from the buses, and the potential requirements of the automobile rental companies have been resolved to minimize movement conflict or delays.

The bent glass plane that defines the western façade endeavors to minimize the structure's scale as it nears the Furness station and to recreate the angle of Walnut Street respective to the city grid. The highly mutable character of the clear glass enclosure permits the movement within the building to activate the city streetscape and uses reflection to enter into a dialogue with the architecture of the station. Movement of buses and trains, along with the varying characterization of the sky, provide a dynamic quality to the surface of the façade. At night, LED lighting and projected imagery on the conference room walls transform the building into a beacon referential to the city and to occasions of celebration.

The silk-screened point-supported glass wall with integral LED displays parallels the Amtrak train platform, and its proximity provides an opportunity for the normally mundane aspects of a parking structure to instead welcome and inform the many travelers and visitors about the movement of trains and relay messages about the city's activities.

The Wilmington Intermodal Transit Center attempts to emulate the forward-thinking spirit in which the Furness station was designed, and, in its quality and refinement, provide both meaning and experiences today.

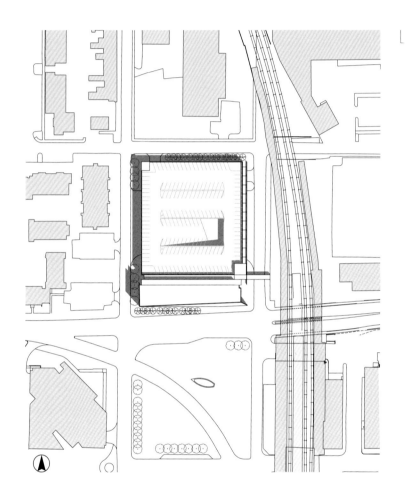

ELSEVIER HEALTH SCIENCES HEADQUARTERS

DESIGN / COMPLETION: 2004 / 2005
LOCATION: PHILADELPHIA, PENNSYLVANIA
CLIENT: ELSEVIER
AREA: 125,000 SQUARE FEET (11,600 SQUARE METERS)

Elsevier, a division of Reed Publications, specializes in scientific, technical, and medical books, journals, and multi-media products and services. A world leader in its field, Elsevier has 7,000 employees in 73 locations around the globe. In addition to book and journal production, Elsevier is also a force in medical "e-publishing," which it sees as a critical part of its future.

In order to house the company's 450 Philadelphia employees, Elsevier leased 125,000 square feet (11,600 square meters) on the top five floors of 4 Penn Center for its new corporate headquarters—a move away from the historical publishing location of Washington Square to a more contemporary setting in Center City. The design of Elsevier's new space responds to the requirements of a younger, technology-savvy employee base. The design challenge was to create an environment that would help recruit and maintain this evolving workforce.

Once a visitor steps onto the reception and executive floor, spatial and visual experiences are tightly controlled. The elevator lobby features dark grey wall coverings printed with subtle characters and numerals, which are discernable only upon close inspection. Three large circular openings in the ceiling plane accommodate primary lighting sources and reinforce the rhythm of elevator door spacing. Glass doors provide secured entries at either end of the elevator lobby. At one end, the doors are only accessed by employees and are faced entirely in an applied graphic film incorporating Elsevier's logo. Visitors naturally move toward the opposite entry, with clear views to the reception space beyond.

The reception occupies a rectangular area that accommodates guest seating, the reception desk, product display, and several collaborative areas. Two primary architectural elements activate the space. A large columnar form stands in front of the curved wall. This element is faced in backlit, translucent resin panels. Three flat-screen monitors, displaying scrolling text and images, are visually suspended in openings created within the surface of the column.

A curving, internally illuminated wall contains displays of printed books and journals and separates more public guest spaces from the semi-public collaborative spaces beyond. The wall's form is analogous to a bound manuscript. The face of the wall is composed of wood slats arranged as pages in a book, while the wall's back surface is a smooth, taut spine. Together, the curved wall and column describe the range of products and services, both print and multi-media, offered by Elsevier today.

DIGITAS WORLD HEADQUARTERS

DESIGN / COMPLETION: 2003 / 2005
LOCATION: BOSTON, MASSACHUSETTS
CLIENT: DIGITAS
AREA: 200,000 SQUARE FEET (18,600 SQUARE METERS)

Boston-based marketing consulting firm Digitas focuses on customer relationship strategy, providing its clients with integrated strategies, technology, and creativity through collaboration, idea generation, and problem solving. In 2005, Digitas relocated its 800 employees to a 200,000-square-foot (18,600-square-meter) space over nine floors of a new high-rise office tower at 33 Arch Street in downtown Boston.

Efficiency, functionality, and fun were the main design drivers for the new space. Client-focused areas including the lobby and presentation rooms were designed to impress visitors with a manifestation of creative design expression and with advanced multimedia technology. Collaboration spaces throughout the Digitas workspace reinforce this initiative.

By design, the plan of the Digitas workspace provides equal quality-of-life amenities to all Digitas employees. In the new headquarters, the percentage of private offices has reduced from 65 to 20 percent. Open workstations are located along the exterior window walls while corridors were planned to allow natural daylight to reach the internal private offices. The space is flooded with daylight views to the outside. Shared meeting rooms are grouped at the middle of the plan immediately adjacent to the elevators, creating a center of energy and activity. Each floor of the Digitas space is based on a universal plan that provides a framework for standardization between floors that is then customized on each floor as necessary to meet unique departmental needs.

The design of the space also includes many sustainable design features. The Digitas space is located in a dense and walkable urban environment. Two subway lines connect immediately adjacent to Digitas, and many employees commute to work using public transportation. Daylight and occupancy sensors automatically dim and switch artificial lighting. Indoor air quality is monitored with CO_2 sensors. Many building materials contain recycled content, and recycling collection is incorporated into the cafeteria and break room millwork. Low-emitting paints, carpets, adhesives, sealants, and composite wood products limit indoor air pollution.

ZHIYE PLAZA OFFICE TOWER

DESIGN / COMPLETION: 2004 / 2006
LOCATION: SUZHOU, CHINA
CLIENT: CHINA-SINGAPORE SUZHOU INDUSTRIAL PARK LAND COMPANY, LTD.
AREA: 538,000 SQUARE FEET (50,000 SQUARE METERS)

The winner of an international design competition, this 538,000-square-foot (50,000-square-meter) office tower represents design predicated on the careful balance of local cultural, environmental, and historical conditions, and the technologically sophisticated requirements of today's office environments. It is respectful to Suzhou's landscape traditions and overtly responsive to its history of waterways and the manner in which they have been interwoven with elements of architecture.

An elegant, memorable, and clear form, the corporate/developer structure defines a new gateway for the administrative district within the 17,300-acre (7,000-hectare) park. The tower and plinth delimit an urban edge and present a grand public entrance to the south, as tradition dictates, while also sheltering an intimate landscaped park and more active entrance to the north. Access to 161,000 square feet (15,000 square meters) of underground parking is carefully incised into this primarily pedestrian environment.

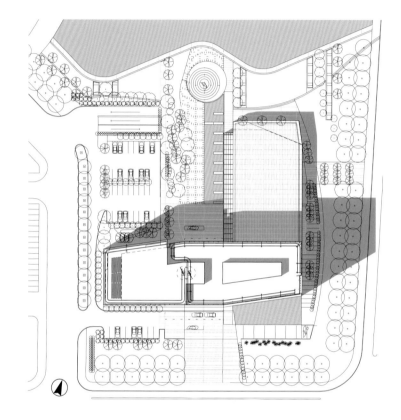

The 18-story slab's enclosure is composed of clear and silk-screened low-E glazing customized for the solar orientation; the south façade adds 12-inch (300-millimeter) sunshades, the east and west orientations employ vertical fins, while the north façade is as planar as possible in response to the plinth's complexity and reflects the adjacent gardens and river. The building vocabulary is one of surfaces and events; balconies, roof extensions, and vertical mesh-covered armatures act as counterpoints to the sheer glass backdrop. The sun, sky, and clouds endlessly repaint the building's surfaces and shift the degrees of transparency and reflectivity. Day or night, the design celebrates the interplay of light and shadow.

A stone rainscreen wall and roof embrace the three-story base that holds areas of dining, exhibition, and congregation. A four-story lobby and three-story linear atrium are the primary public spaces and are predicated on views to the outside where linear reflecting pools, fountains, planting, and stone reinterpret the area's gardens. Tensile-structured curtain walls and polished floors, soffits, and interior walls that create layers of reflectivity intentionally blend boundaries between natural and constructed environments.

The realized facility is at the forefront of office design within this rapidly growing international city.

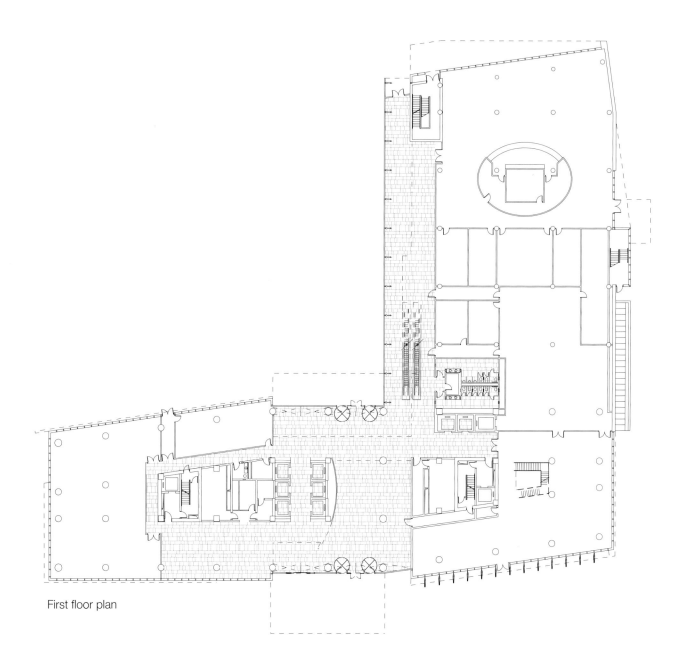

First floor plan

294   Zhiye Plaza Office Tower

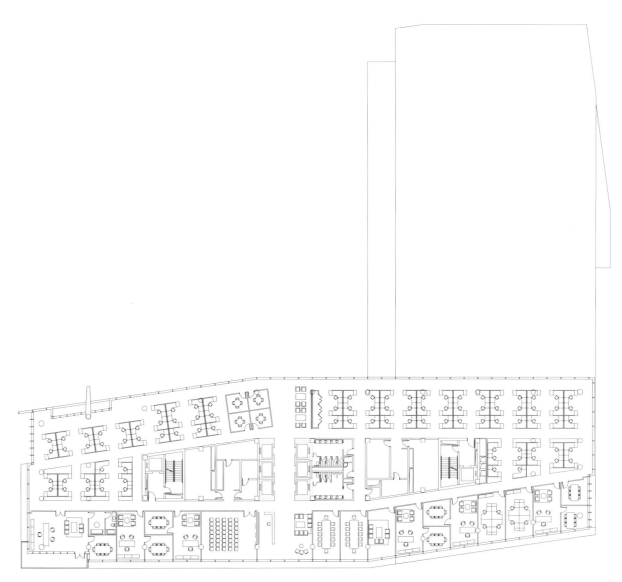

Typical tower floor plan

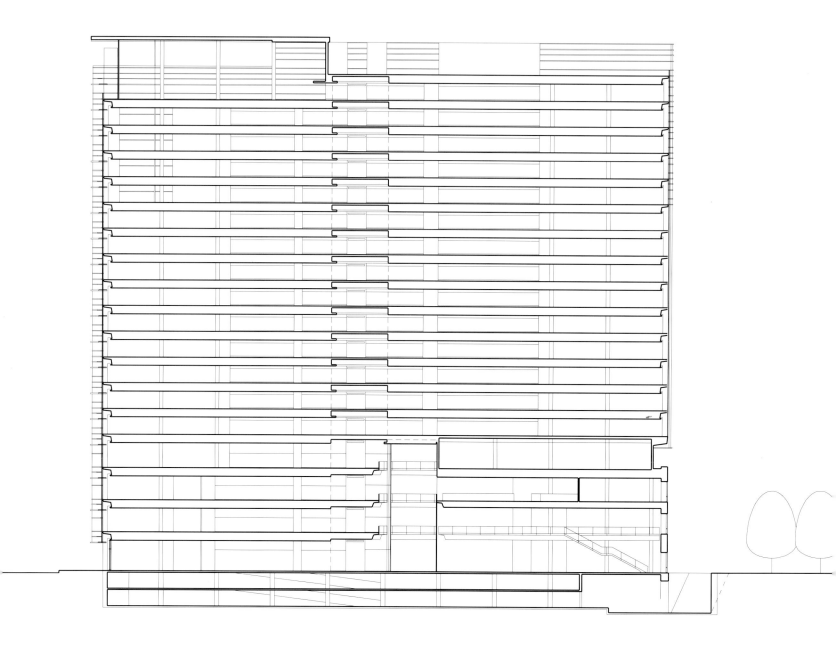

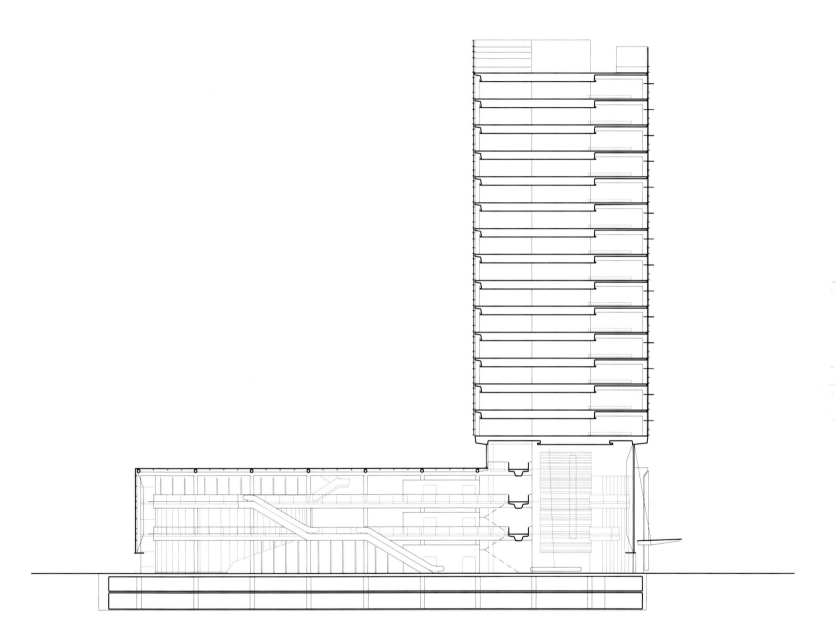

302   Zhiye Plaza Office Tower

312   Zhiye Plaza Office Tower

SAP COMPETITION

DESIGN: 2006
LOCATION: NEWTOWN SQUARE, PENNSYLVANIA
CLIENT: SAP AMERICA, INC.
AREA: 400,000 SQUARE FEET (37,200 SQUARE METERS)

SAP America requested concepts for a master plan development that would provide incremental growth in two phases of 200,000 square feet (18,600 square meters) each as an addition to the 425,000-square-foot (39,500-square-meter) headquarters building that was completed in 1999. Beyond the additional office area, SAP desired campus corporate housing for visiting executives and a corporate conference center separate from the office facilities. The criteria included consideration for the corporate culture, respect for the existing natural environment, environmental consciousness, and availability of a long-term investment exit strategy.

The proposed design was predicated on a respect for the character of the site and a minimization of the impact that new development would have on both the natural environment, and also the conditions and views presently enjoyed by SAP's employees. The envisioned new campus would be planned to promote creativity and collaboration, so the issues of circulation and physical ramifications were important.

The design proposed two long, narrow, fractured rectangles that nestled in the gradually sloping terrain before each transitioned into dense woodland. A ground-level sheltered link joined the first phase with the existing building and became a treetop bridge as it connected to the second structure. The termination of this hovering bridge was the conference center 60 feet (18 meters) below the entrance elevation. Both the buildings and the connector touched lightly on the existing topography.

Clad entirely in clear and silk-screened glass, the new office structures were to effect a presence more about the surrounding environment than about a statement of architecture. While a sheer glass façade defined the north faces, a three-dimensional brise-soleil provided protection from solar gain on the south. Chamfered façades lessened the building's perceived bulk in relation to the surrounding trees, while bringing the reflection of the sky more into the composition.

The conference center was carefully integrated into a clearing within the forest, adjacent to a small existing pond, and proximal to the small-scaled housing placed carefully within this wooded depression. The residences were primarily vertical to minimize their impact and were characterized by wooden shutters and dark green cladding to blend with the surrounding conditions.

The design specifics included green roofs, gray water conservation, passive and active solar controls, recycled materials, and utilization of locally manufactured products. The expectation was to achieve a minimum of LEED® Gold Certification, with the collective aspiration to achieve Platinum Certification.

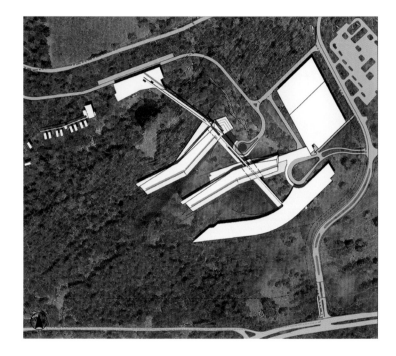

318 SAP Competition

UNIVERSITY OF COLORADO HEALTH SCIENCES CENTER, RC2

(IN ASSOCIATION WITH FENTRESS ARCHITECTS)

DESIGN / COMPLETION: 2006 / 2008
LOCATION: AURORA, COLORADO
CLIENT: UNIVERSITY OF COLORADO AT DENVER AND HEALTH SCIENCES CENTER
SQUARE FOOTAGE: 500,000 SQUARE FEET (46,500 SQUARE METERS)

Research Complex 2 of the University of Colorado Health Sciences Center is a 507,000-square-foot (46,500-square-meter), 12-story building that defines, in concert with an academic office structure to the south, the western edge of a 4-acre (1.6-hectare) landscaped courtyard. Linked by second-floor bridges that form a public grand promenade and sheltered by arcades at grade, the four buildings that delimit this quadrangle are organized to facilitate collaboration and are designed to reinforce the orchestrated dialogue between architecture and landscape architecture.

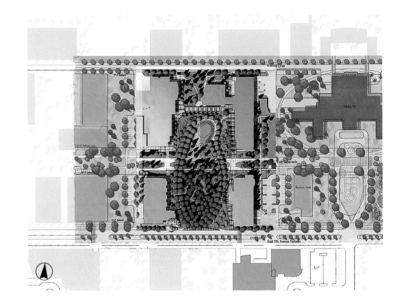

The building is primarily planned around a prototypical laboratory environment accompanied by adjacent flexible support space. These elements constitute the western two-thirds of each floor, with office areas occupying a parallel zone to the east. Providing a measure of flexibility on each floor, the north and south laboratory zones are programmed to operate either as labs or offices, dictated by the needs of the specific department.

A primary public circulation path joins the offices and areas of congregation. Distinct from this, and encapsulated within the secure laboratory barrier, a linear equipment corridor provides both access to the labs as well as space for supporting equipment, thereby lessening noise within the research suites. Although composed from a set of standard parts, each floor is able to respond to the specific requirements of the twenty university departments that will be in residence.

The architectural character has been greatly informed by both the immediate context and regional considerations. Brick, sympathetic to existing structures and the color of the earth, encases the laboratory areas; the framed window punctuations provide expansive views of the Rockies while sheltering the occupants from the western sun. The offices exist behind a highly articulated, clear and silk-screened, high-performance curtain wall that has been detailed as three overlapping planes, each of which evolve as they progress from north to south. Within the glass façade, internal events, including the two-story interaction areas, are telegraphed to the outside. Mullion profiles and depths, fins, and patterns form an active and ever-changing backdrop to the courtyard. Between these two treatments are metal panels that define areas of technical support and building systems and culminate expressively in the mechanical penthouse.

While endeavoring to be a testament to the virtues of modern architecture and an expression of the technology within, the design of UCDHSC Research Complex 1 and 2 is, above all else, about the creation of an environment contributory to scientific discovery.

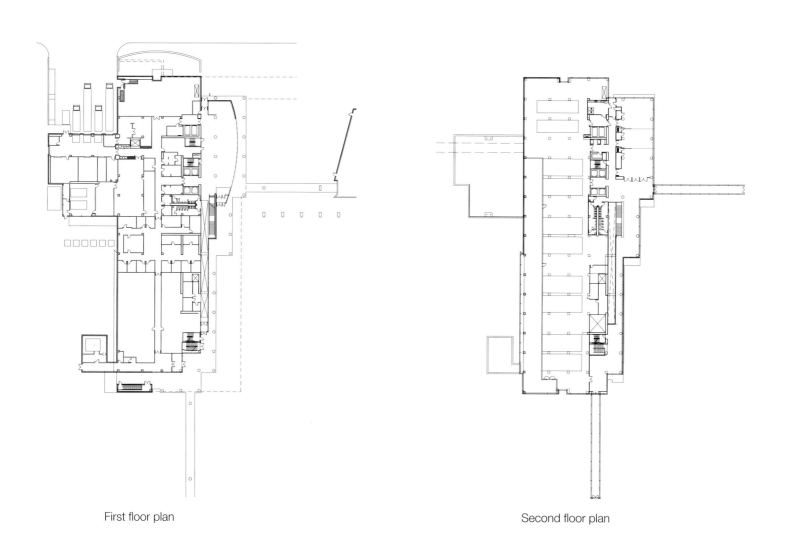

First floor plan

Second floor plan

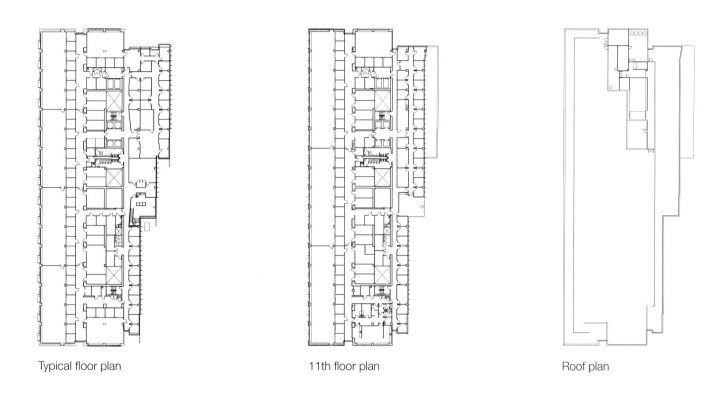

Typical floor plan

11th floor plan

Roof plan

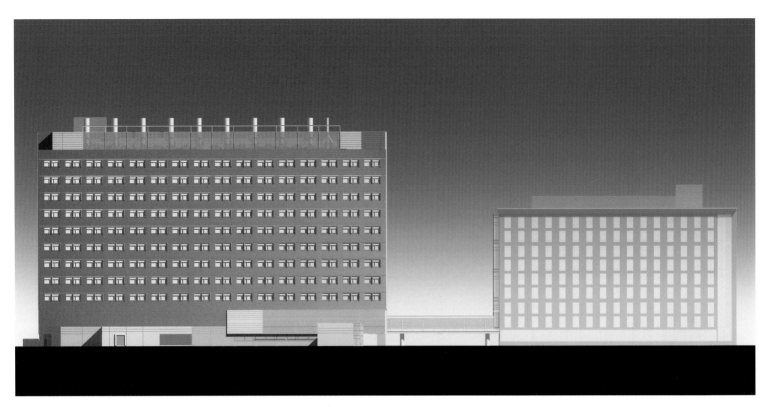

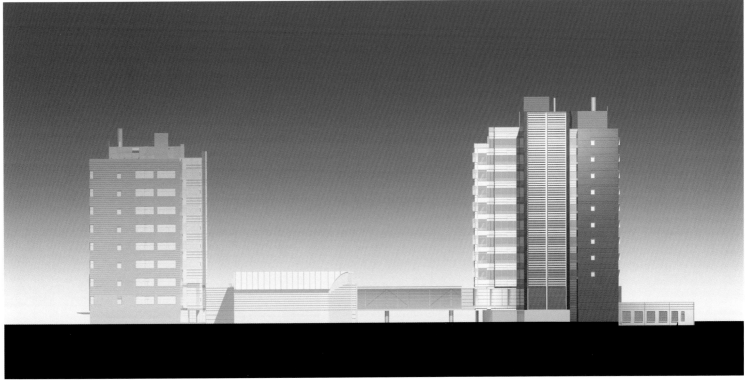

University of Colorado Health Sciences Center, RC2

ROCKEFELLER UNIVERSITY COMPARATIVE BIOSCIENCE CENTER ANNEX

DESIGN / COMPLETION: 2007 / 2009
LOCATION: NEW YORK, NEW YORK
CLIENT: ROCKEFELLER UNIVERSITY
AREA: 29,000 SQUARE FEET (2,700 SQUARE METERS)

In 2006, The Rockefeller University, a private institution focusing primarily on post-graduate biomedical research, planned to consolidate its behavioral research facilities to the south section of its campus onto a 40-foot-wide (12-meter) sliver of property nestled between existing buildings. The University, situated between 63rd and 68th Streets on Manhattan's bustling Upper East Side, was founded in 1901 by John D. Rockefeller as a Research Institute that began to encompass education in 1965. Rockefeller boasts associations with 23 Nobel Prize winners and multiple scientific breakthroughs that have enhanced our lives.

The solution to this urban infill became a multi-story building constrained by the two adjacent research facilities, an existing loading area, numerous site utilities, two subway and two train tunnels, a pedestrian sidewalk at 63rd Street, and by the need to be contextually sensitive to a recently completed suspension pedestrian bridge that links the research buildings to faculty housing.

Despite it being smaller than other buildings on campus, Rockefeller University wanted the new research annex to have a significant visual presence—both to 63rd Street and also facing north toward its internal multi-level landscaped plaza. With this in mind, the building has been designed as a simple rectilinear prism to contrast with the Brutalist character of the adjacent buildings. Layered with bright silver metal panels that are articulated in symphony with the adjacent buildings' joint patterns, the solid mass of the building is further diffused by the curtain wall at the south façade that adds a layer of transparency and reflectivity that presents to students, faculty, and the public the most recent manifestation of the University's ongoing mission of investigation.

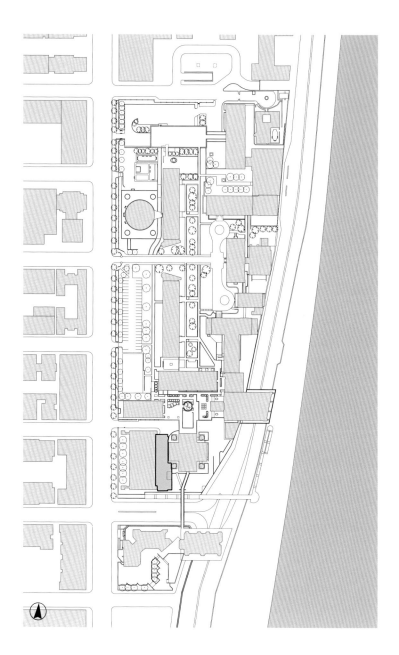

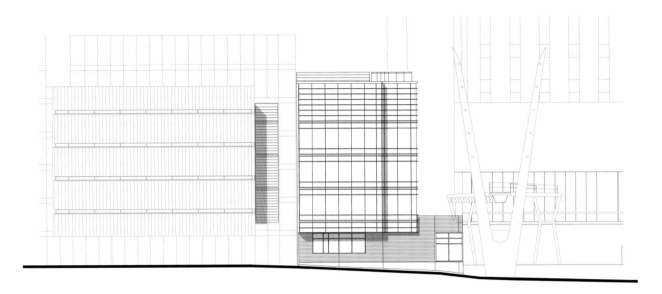

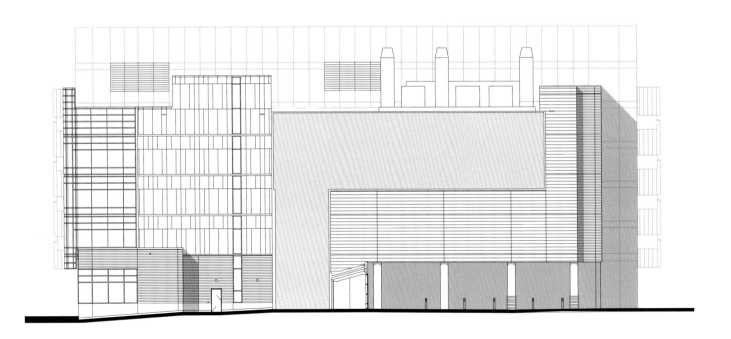

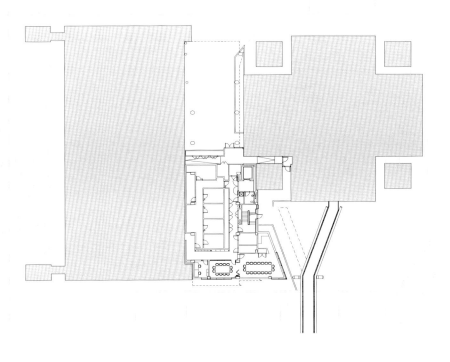

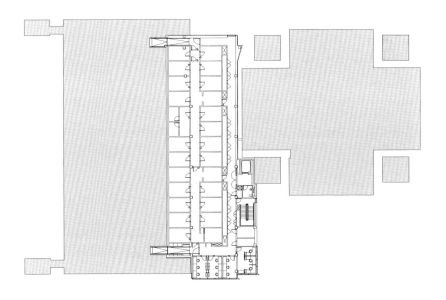

LINCOLN UNIVERSITY NEW SCIENCE / HIGH TECHNOLOGY BUILDING

DESIGN / COMPLETION: 2006 / 2008
LOCATION: CHESTER COUNTY, PENNSYLVANIA
CLIENT: LINCOLN UNIVERSITY
AREA: 125,000 SQUARE FEET (11,600 SQUARE METERS)

Lincoln University's Science and General Classroom High Technology Building is the most recent physical enhancement to America's first historically Black University. Integral to the continued success of the science-based and liberal arts core curriculum, the new facility is envisioned as critical to the university's mission of providing its 2,000 students the appropriate resources to achieve an education that remains abreast of technological and cultural change.

The new 125,000-square-foot (11,600-square-meter) science building is to be the first element within a new quadrangle south of the main campus. It has been sited to define the eastern boundary of the planned academic development, and to take advantage of expansive views from its position at the top of a gradually sloped meadow. Its placement and configuration are respectful of an adjacent stand of mature trees, and informed by optimal pedestrian and vehicular circulation.

Programmatically, the building has been designed to house the teaching and faculty requirements of the chemistry, biology, physics, mathematics, and computer science departments. Teaching and research laboratories, classrooms, tutorial spaces, and departmental offices have been planned for optimal flexibility in the future, and with overt regard to the interaction dynamics between students and faculty members. The corridors that separate the classrooms from the professors' offices are understood in terms of the requirements for circulation, but even more so for their promotion of interaction.

The two wings of the three-story building correspond to the program of the five departments and the university-wide teaching spaces. Teaching spaces are across from the corresponding departmental offices, and all areas are infused with daylight and provided with carefully framed views. The juncture between the wings is utilized as the student lounge and auditoria breakout space on the ground floor and a double-height faculty lounge that links all departments above.

The two primary exterior façades are clad in red brick, sympathetic to the existing campus fabric. The internal masonry walls that define the courtyards and atrium are sheathed in a gray iron spot brick that better reflects light and is a fitting reflection of the technological program contained within. Black aluminum framing reinforces the rhythmic aspects of the fenestration—voids within the walls, as opposed to simply windows. Within the interior, polished concrete and concrete block, wood paneling, and clear glass are played against a broad palette of color on the doors and their surrounds.

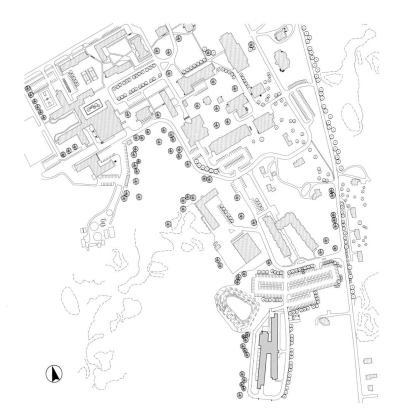

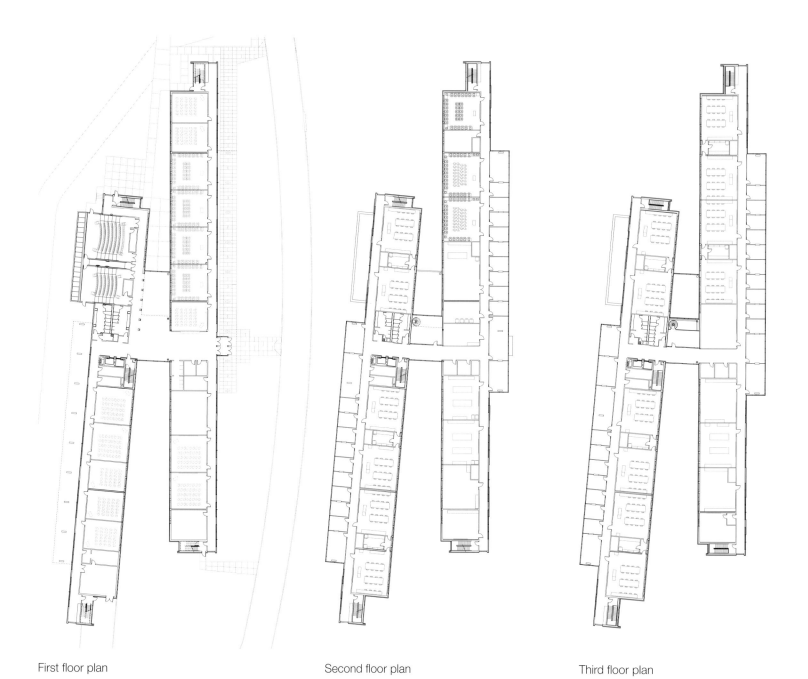

First floor plan   Second floor plan   Third floor plan

AMGEN HELIX CAMPUS EXPANSION PLAN

DESIGN / COMPLETION: 2007 /
LOCATION: SEATTLE, WASHINGTON
CLIENT: AMGEN
AREA: 1,200,000 SQUARE FEET ON 40 ACRES (111,000 SQUARE METERS ON 16 HECTARES)

Overlooking downtown Seattle and Elliott Bay, Amgen's Helix Campus houses the company's drug discovery process in a unique and spectacular setting. This expansion plan seeks to balance several dynamic and contemporary new buildings with more traditional existing structures and the site's extensive open spaces and waterfront. Four of the new buildings house laboratories and research spaces in a double-loaded "racetrack" configuration alongside administrative areas concentrated in a four-story loft environment. These 135,000-square-foot (12,500-square-meter) structures are sited to maximize exposure to the surrounding mountain scenery including a particularly clear view of Mt. Rainier. At the end of 16th Avenue West, a new administrative/ amenity structure will serve as both the new visitor "front door" and the primary employee commons. This building will also anchor a new landscaped quadrangle that serves as a central focus of the expanded campus.

The architectural design of the proposed facilities aims to integrate old with new. With the overall Helix Campus expansion planned to be completed in phases, each new structure will be designed to complement the existing campus environment, maximizing the open spaces and exceptional views offered by the unique site setting. Contemporary buildings that combine metal panel and glass with masonry accents will reference both the current site vocabulary and local maritime environment. The general ideals of the campus layout including sense of flow, flexibility, safety, and environmental awareness, will translate into the built environment. The new work spaces will foster an increase in collaboration and cross-communication, assisting in an improved and enjoyable working environment.

The interior design will vary, as each facility's design will cater to the specific function of the building (such as lab, amenity, office). An overall interior design concept will additionally reflect the broader campus goals of increased communication, collaboration, safety, and site awareness. Racetrack corridor circulation will be used to increase flow while open floor plans in offices and laboratories will promote teamwork and enhance flexibility.

A visitor's entrance will be installed by the new administration building, improving site security and organization. Site planning and landscape design for the expansion will enhance employee and visitor experiences, both accentuating the natural features of the site and incorporating the existing campus facilities. Canopies are included in building designs to provide shelter while pedestrian walkways, both open-air ground level and enclosed elevated, will serve as connectors to the various buildings and encourage employee interaction.

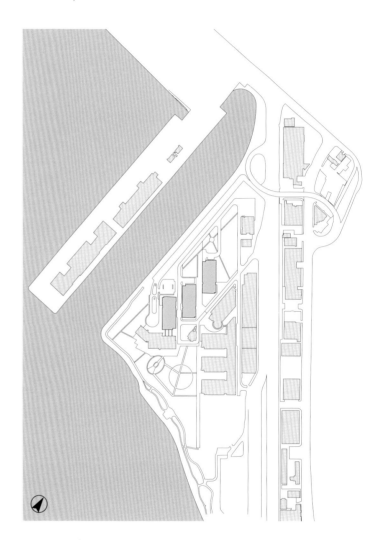

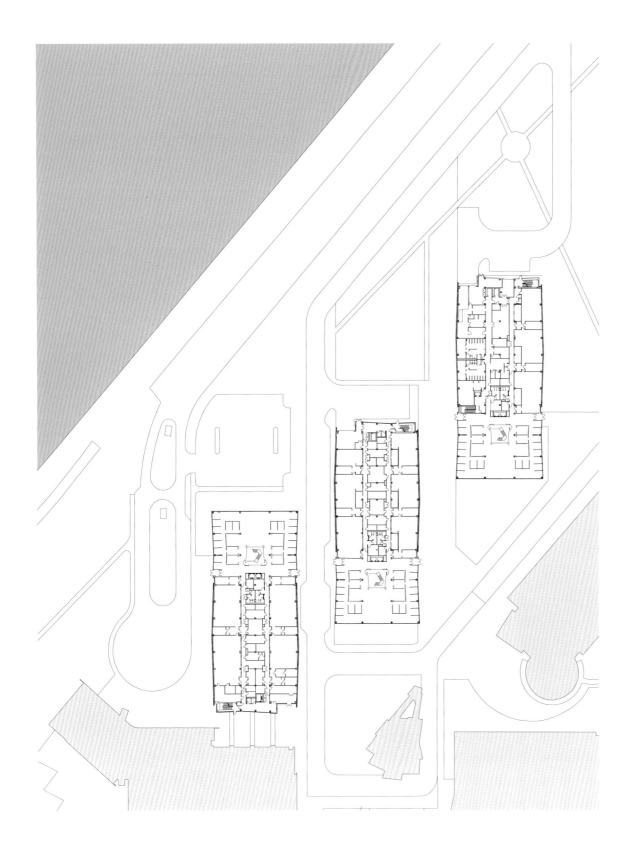

350   Amgen Helix Campus Expansion Plan

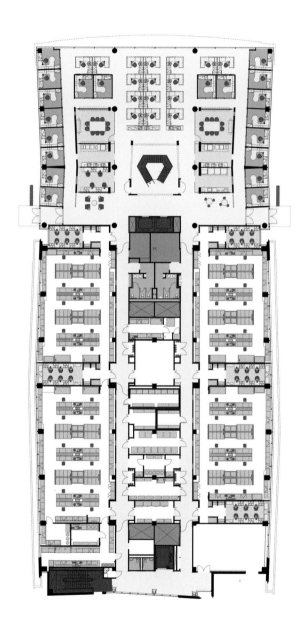
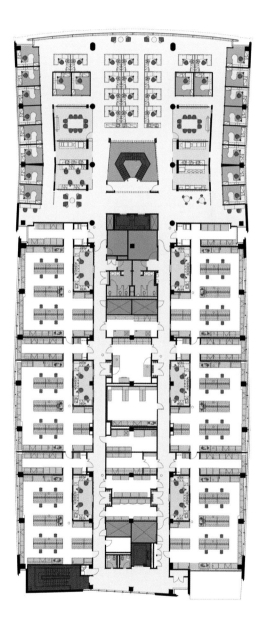

Amgen Helix Campus Expansion Plan 351

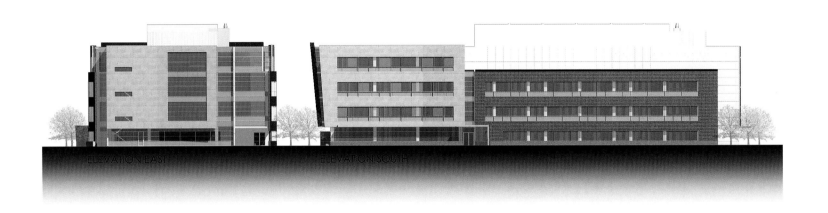

ELEVATION EAST ELEVATION SOUTH

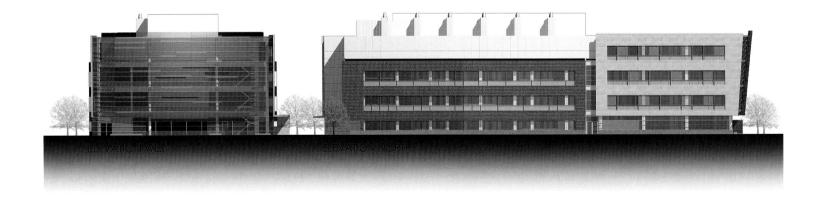

ELEVATION WEST ELEVATION NORTH

DRUG ENFORCEMENT ADMINISTRATION CLANDESTINE LAB

DESIGN / COMPLETION: 2006 / 2008
LOCATION: QUANTICO, VIRGINIA
CLIENT: US NAVY
AREA: 32,000 SQUARE FEET (3,000 SQUARE METERS)

A varied and intense set of programs is captured in the new laboratory and training facility for the Drug Enforcement Administration (DEA) at Quantico: drug demonstration laboratories, raid training rooms, and teaching classrooms. The challenge was to create a dramatic and sculptural container that related to adjacent buildings while isolating conditions for internal needs.

Analytical and mock labs seek to replicate the environments and processes used in actual clandestine drug production rings. Physical training spaces include both smoke-filled and acoustically isolated raid simulation rooms with viewing mezzanines, firearms-automated training system spaces, padded physical training rooms, and equipment and clothing try-on spaces. Other educational training facilities include classrooms. Additional support spaces include an administrative suite for housing of up to 26 staff, conference room, multi-purpose room, break room/vending, and shower and laundry facilities.

Spaces are organized around a gracious two-story central spine, which allows daylight throughout the length of the building and serves as a breakout area for several of the training spaces. The design of the roofscape was of primary importance since a neighboring DEA training facility overlooks the building. A lower-level overhang provides shelter for outdoor training space; an opening in the overhang offers daylight to a lounge area. The intersection of the overhang with an elevated roof meets at the central spine to create the elegant clerestory.

In addition, the facility meets anti-terrorism and force protection requirements, is designed to resist tremors from nearby mortar fire, incorporates a central mechanical mezzanine, and is served by both redundant mechanical systems (chillers) and emergency power.

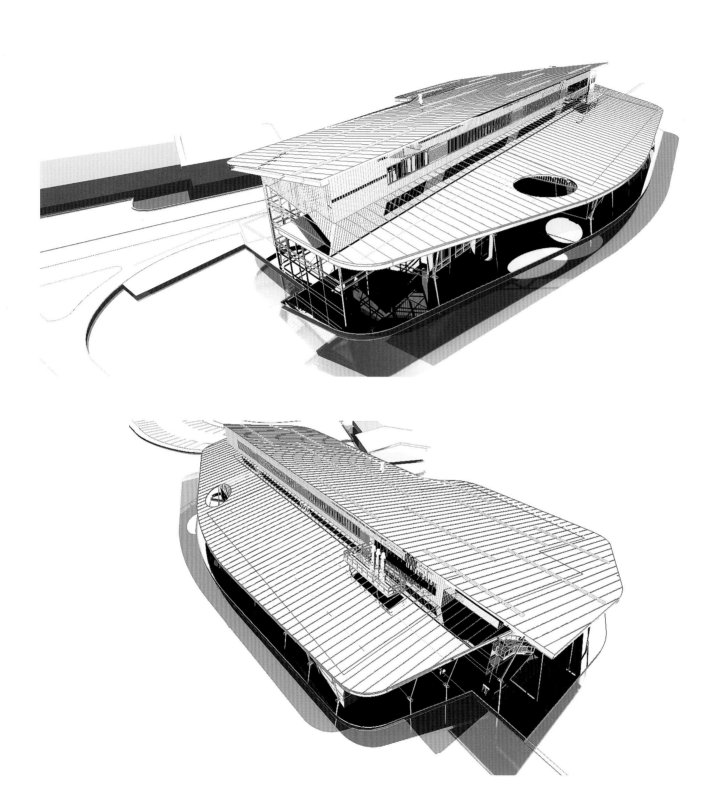

Drug Enforcement Administration Clandestine Lab

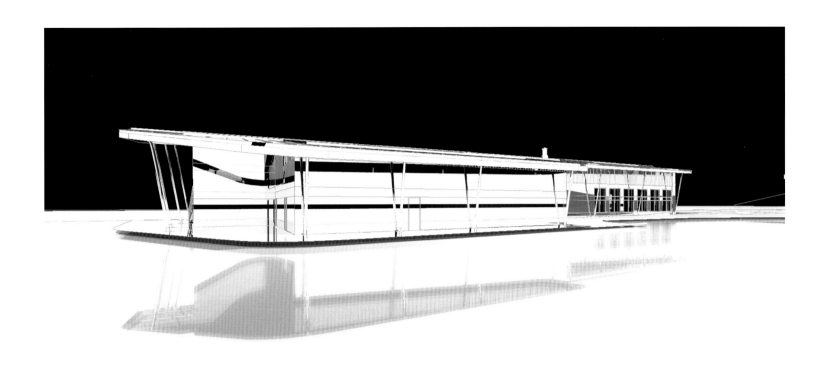

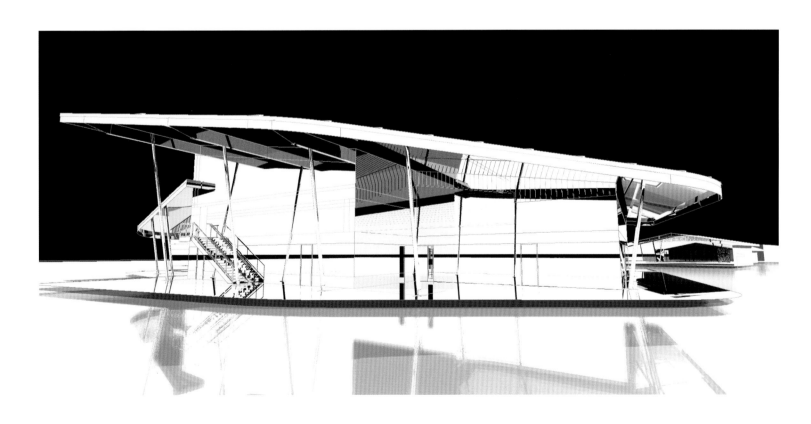

US FDA HEADQUARTERS CONSOLIDATION – CENTRAL SHARED USE FACILITY
(IN ASSOCIATION WITH RTKL)

DESIGN / COMPLETION: 2004 / 2006
LOCATION: WHITE OAK, MARYLAND
CLIENT: GENERAL SERVICES ADMINISTRATION
AREA: 137,000 SQUARE FEET (12,700 SQUARE METERS)

As the third phase of the Food and Drug Administration (FDA) White Oak campus implementation, the Central Shared Use (CSU) building is the symbolic heart of the campus. Paired with the former main Naval Ordnance Laboratory administration building (Building One), the CSU is the main arrival space for the campus, creating the new identity for the FDA. Employees and visitors arrive in a newly created forecourt, then pass through a new lobby beneath the historic building and arrive at a monumental atrium in the CSU building, with views out onto the campus commons and woodlands beyond. Programmatically, the CSU building plays a key role in realizing the consolidation effort, physically bringing together the four distinct centers of the FDA through shared amenities such as dining, training, fitness center, health services, I.T. services, and the FDA library. A two-story circulation spine connects the north and south sides of the campus, linking the campus-wide pedestrian arteries. This 300-foot-long (91-meter) gallery will be the site of a major work of public art to be commissioned under the GSA Arts in Architecture program. The transparent east façade facing the main commons is designed to reveal the activities and artwork inside and provide views to the landscaped commons and woodland beyond. The other three façades are clad in brick, complementing the existing brick and limestone of the historic Building One.

As the most public building on the FDA campus, the CSU was seen as an opportunity to make sustainable design visible to the employees and visitors. While all buildings on the FDA campus are being designed to meet LEED® Certification criteria, the CSU has been designed to establish a new benchmark for the campus. This effort led to the inclusion of the following strategies: increased use of daylighting, sun shading devices optimized by digital solar modeling, natural thermosiphon ventilation of the atrium and primary circulation spaces (including use of operable windows), thermal mass (with night flushing), and a green roof. These strategies emphasize working with natural systems, climate, and microclimate to reduce energy use and provide water quality and quantity management. They complement the sustainable design strategy being implemented campus-wide, features of which include a central co-generation plant, economizer cycles, high-efficiency lighting, low-flow plumbing fixtures, and building commissioning.

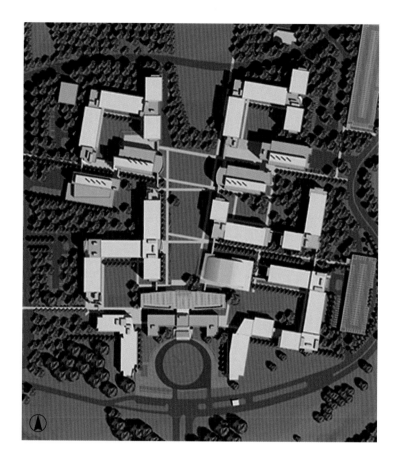

INTERNATIONAL EXPO AND RETAIL CENTER

DESIGN: 2006
LOCATION: BAKU, AZERBAIJAN
CLIENT: JSC CROCUS INTERNATIONAL
AREA: 862,000 SQUARE FEET (80,100 SQUARE METERS)

Located in Baku, the capital and largest city of Azerbaijan, this project was commissioned by JSC Crocus International on behalf of the First Lady of Azerbaijan, Mehriban Aliyeva. The program calls for two distinct components: a 344,000-square-foot (32,000-square meter) International Expo Center and 517,000 square feet (48,000 square meters) of retail space for Tvoi Dom, a Moscow-based 24-hour department store that stocks more than 300,000 different products ranging from gardening and construction supplies to groceries and lifestyle products. This project is situated 2.2 miles (3.5 kilometers) from the International Airport along the main highway to the historical center of Baku. As such, the Baku International Expo and Retail Center is ideally situated not only to serve the needs of the local population but also to promote Baku's role as a center of business and commerce in the greater Caucasus region.

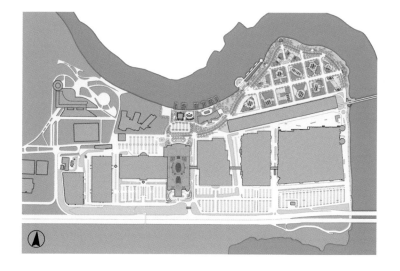

The design is concerned with the two complementary yet distinct program types addressing the scale of the highway. The forms for these elements respond specifically to different functional demands: the inward focus of Tvoi Dom is reflected in a façade that is concave and mostly opaque, and the externally focused character of the Expo Center is manifest by a transparent convex glass lobby expressive of technology. Taken together these forms create a sinuous unifying gesture that functions at the highway scale and animates the 2,100-foot-long (650-meter) façade. A LED signage tower, the only vertical element on the site, and a distinctive LED-accented curved roof are additional elements that function at the scale of the highway.

Internally, the planning of the Expo halls is rational and efficient. There are two 118,000-square-foot (11,000-square-meter) halls separated by an operable partition and the 89- by 98-foot (27- by 30-meter) structural bay spacing works with the typical 10- by 10-foot (3- by 3-meter) exhibitor module. Support functions are housed in a 59-foot-thick (18-meter) wall separating the lobby from the Expo halls. In contrast to the polished steel and glass of the exterior, this wall between the lobby and Expo halls is constructed of limestone, the traditional building material of ancient Baku.

JSC CROCUS INTERNATIONAL RESORT, THE RIVIERA

DESIGN / COMPLETION: 2005 / 2010
LOCATION: MOSCOW, RUSSIA
CLIENT: JSC CROCUS INTERNATIONAL
AREA: 2,900,000 SQUARE FEET (269,000 SQUARE METERS)

Envisioned as a symbolic landmark on the skyline, JSC Crocus International's 210-acre (85-hectare) mixed-use development is sited directly along the Moscow River. The Riviera site defines the heart of the campus, with a dense concentration of diverse uses. The Riviera itself is a spatially rich urban complex that creatively integrates a casino, 635-room luxury hotel, and a major classically themed retail environment into a destination facility that is unique in Russia.

The complex unites the diverse facilities of the Crocus campus: two major retail malls to the south, three major Expo convention halls, and a major commercial office, hotel, and residence zone to the north. The entire campus will be connected via conditioned sky concourses to the multiple-level retail environment that will serve as the prime indoor public assembly place, complete with navigable canals, piazzas, and a vaulted sky ceiling.

Below the elevated retail podium is a full-level gaming floor containing a sports book zone, table slot areas, and a VIP gaming room supported by restaurants, cafes, and bars, and adjacent to the major rotunda and the hotel lobbies. Directly above the retail environment are a sky-lit rooftop pool, spa, performance space, and garden.

The rotunda space is a double-stacked dome, with the lower one enclosing a 115-foot-high (35-meter) entry lobby with vertical circulation connecting gaming to all retail and cinema levels. Its cupola penetrates through the 98-foot (30-meter) upper dome that contains a high-end nightclub. The outer dome drum acts as a performance stage and backdrop, as needed.

Visually, The Riviera extends the world of thematically inspired architecture that exists in the adjacent Crocus Mall, and has been influenced by the historical fabric of center city Moscow. Highly profiled stone is envisioned for the podium, while a sophisticated, high-performance glass and stone curtain wall system have been designed for the hotel tower.

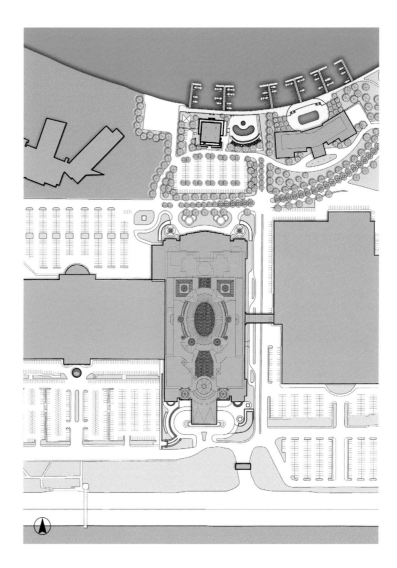

JSC CROCUS INTERNATIONAL

DESIGN: 2007
LOCATION: MOSCOW, RUSSIA
CLIENT: JSC CROCUS INTERNATIONAL
AREA: 10,800,000 SQUARE FEET (1,000,000 SQUARE METERS)

In the fall of 2006, Aras Agalarov, President of JSC Crocus International, commissioned the development of a master plan and conceptual design for a mixed-use development of 13 individual towers totaling more than 10,800,000 square feet (1,000,000 square meters) of built space. Inspired by Mr. Agalarov's own experience living in New York City, the development is designed to emulate the density, vibrancy, and high fashion of Madison Avenue. Urban planning issues have organized the development, while pedestrian movement, vehicular movement, and infrastructure design have provided governance. A desire for the typical diversity of a city environment evolved over time and has given form to the district of office towers, hotels, and high-end condominiums. This development is called "Manhattan."

Located on 57 acres (23 hectares) of land fronting the Moscow River, "Manhattan" is part of a larger master plan developed in 2005 for JSC Crocus International. In total, JSC Crocus International controls 210 acres (85 hectares) along the outermost ring road surrounding Moscow, the MKAD, on which it had originally developed a 24-hour hypermarket (Tvoi Dom), a boutique mall, a yacht club, and a 3,230,000-square-foot (300,000-square-meter) exposition center. A 600-room casino–hotel and themed retail mall is currently under development for this site.

To capture the vitality and variety of Manhattan, there are 13 individual blocks for 13 individual towers. A block size of 246 x 262 feet (75 x 80 meters) was chosen because it provides a finer grain at the street level while being large enough to support a typical tower footprint. The placement, massing, and orientation of the towers relates to the Moscow River frontage. The smaller, more intimately scaled condominiums and hotels are placed along the river's edge while the taller office towers terrace upwards and back from this edge to the center of the site.

Without a true end-user client, the design of the towers, by necessity, fell into several lines of investigation. One series was based in differing extrapolations of a hexagonal floor plate. Office Tower 6 and Hotel Tower 7 explored forms derived from an exploration of sustainable building systems inherent in connected atria. There were also designs that were more pictorial in origin—the twisting form of Tower 1 and the sinuous and overlapping curves of the paired condominiums at parcels 12 and 13.

All of the buildings along "Madison Avenue" have commercial bases designed to accommodate the fashion industry, which Crocus plays host to in its retail and exposition facilities.

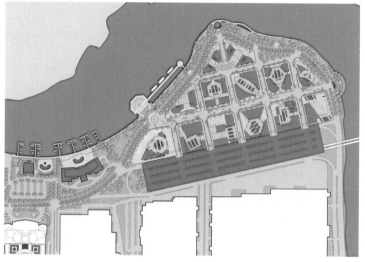

TOWER 12+13

Floors	33
Height	117m

Podium	12,400m2
Tower	60,300m2
Total	72,700m2

TOWER 11

Floors	37
Height	165m

Podium	6,800m2
Tower	35,600m2
Total	42,400m2

TOWER 7

Floors	42
Height	152m

Podium	6,900m2
Tower	45,200m2
Total	52,100m2

TOWER 2

Floors	37
Height	165m

Podium	11,100m2
Tower	55,600m2
Total	66,700m2

TOWER 1

Floors	44
Height	188m

Podium	9,300m2
Tower	99,600m2
Total	108,900m2

TOWER 5

Floors	49
Height	220m

Podium	13,600m2
Tower	84,600m2
Total	98,200m2

TOWER 10

Floors	48
Height	220m

Podium	8,000m2
Tower	72,700m2
Total	80,700m2

TOWER 8

Floors	47
Height	220m

Podium	9,100m2
Tower	73,200m2
Total	82,300m2

TOWER 9

Floors	55
Height	242m

Podium	9,200m2
Tower	92,300m2
Total	101,500m2

TOWER 6

Floors	62
Height	248m

Podium	9,100m2
Tower	109,100m2
Total	118,200m2

TOWER 3

Floors	50
Height	255m

Podium	8,500m2
Tower	94,500m2
Total	103,000m2

TOWER 4

Floors	70
Height	310m

Podium	12,100m2
Tower	99,300m2
Total	111,400m2

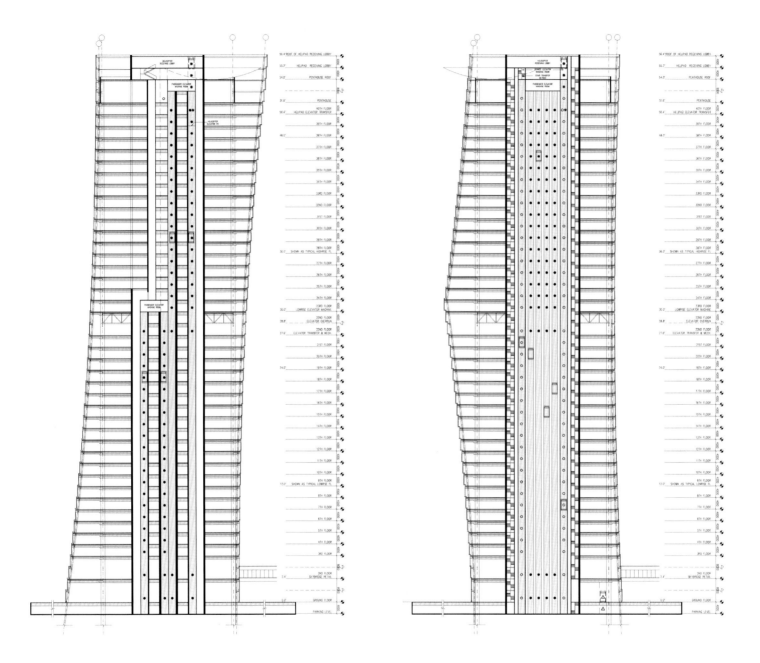

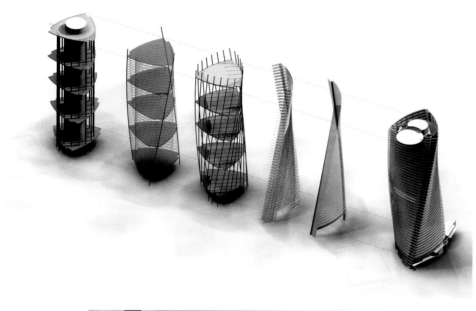

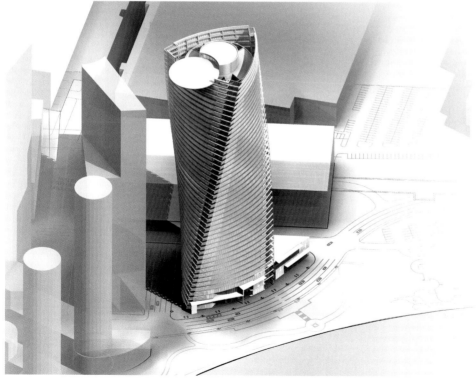

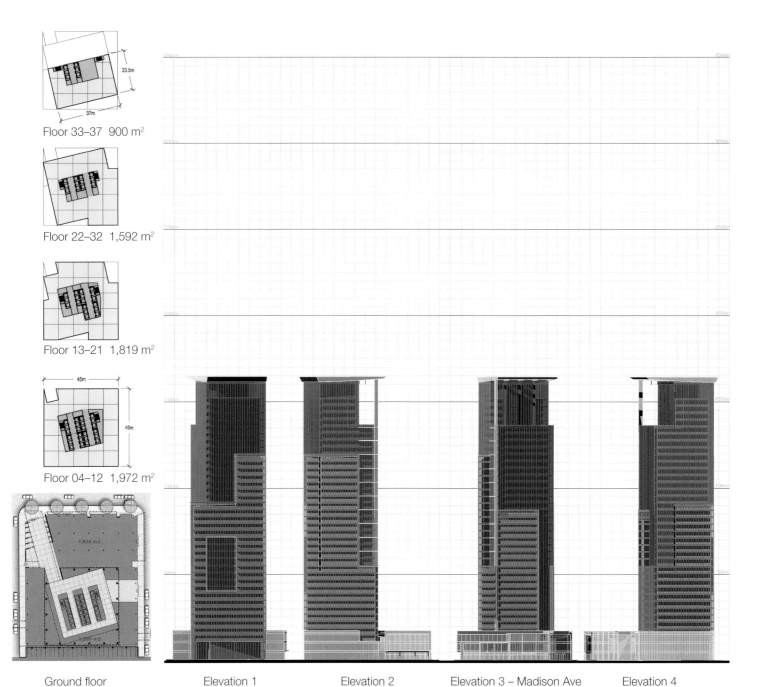

Floor 33–37 900 m²

Floor 22–32 1,592 m²

Floor 13–21 1,819 m²

Floor 04–12 1,972 m²

Ground floor

Elevation 1

Elevation 2

Elevation 3 – Madison Ave

Elevation 4

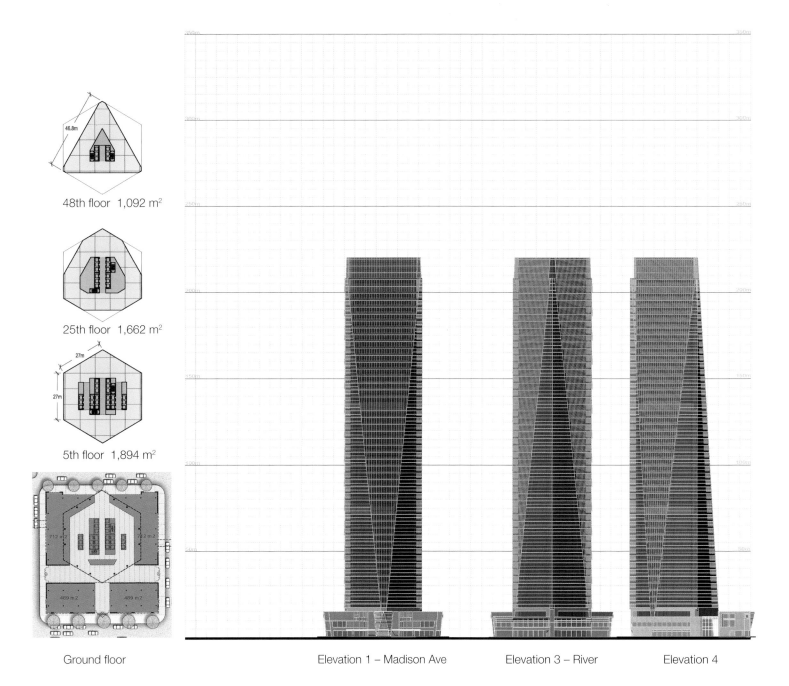

48th floor 1,092 m²

25th floor 1,662 m²

5th floor 1,894 m²

Ground floor

Elevation 1 – Madison Ave

Elevation 3 – River

Elevation 4

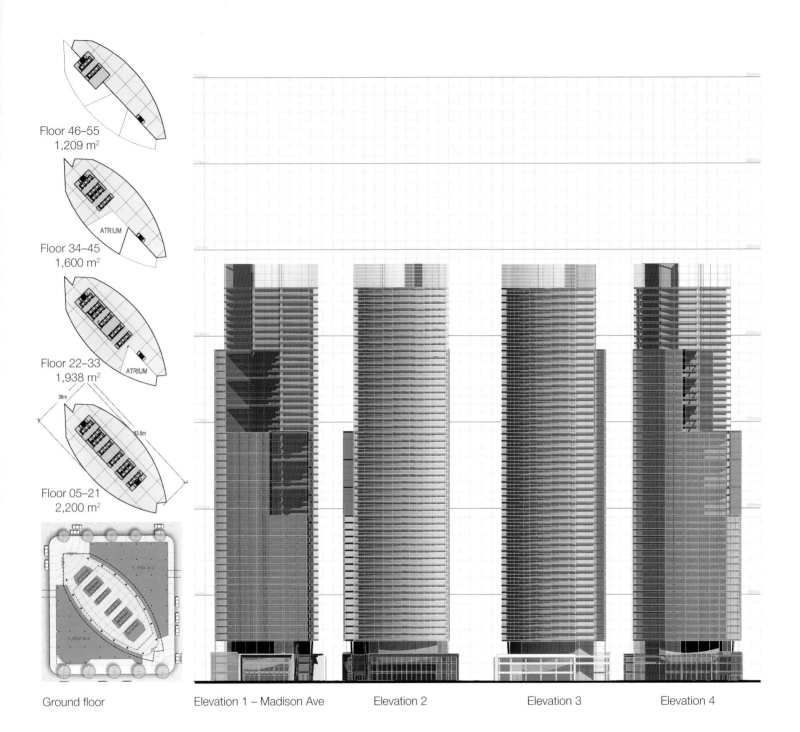

Floor 46–55
1,209 m²

Floor 34–45
1,600 m²

ATRIUM

Floor 22–33
1,938 m²

ATRIUM

36m

93.8m

Floor 05–21
2,200 m²

1,359 m²

1,062 m²

Ground floor

Elevation 1 – Madison Ave

Elevation 2

Elevation 3

Elevation 4

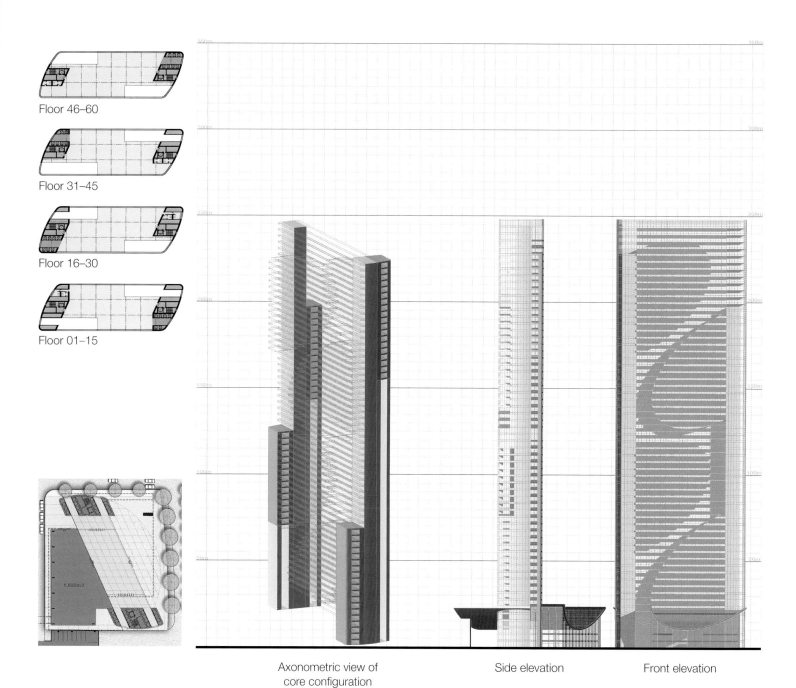

Floor 46–60

Floor 31–45

Floor 16–30

Floor 01–15

1,505m2

Axonometric view of
core configuration

Side elevation

Front elevation

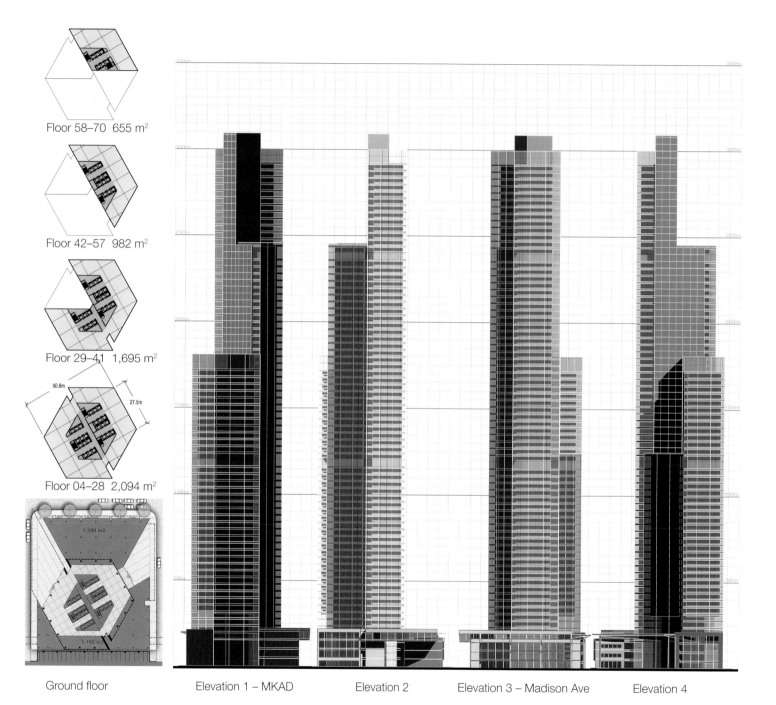

Floor 58–70 655 m²

Floor 42–57 982 m²

Floor 29–41 1,695 m²

50.8m

27.5m

Floor 04–28 2,094 m²

1,320 m2

1,165 m2

Ground floor

Elevation 1 – MKAD

Elevation 2

Elevation 3 – Madison Ave

Elevation 4

GUANGZHOU PEARL RIVER TOWERS

DESIGN: 2007
LOCATION: GUANGZHOU, CHINA
CLIENT: POLY REAL ESTATE CO., LTD. AND XIANCUN ECONOMIC AND DEVELOPMENT COMPANY
AREA: 1,520,000 SQUARE FEET (141,000 SQUARE METERS)

The conceptual study for the new mixed-use commercial complex in Pearl River New City is an example of China's continuing and accelerated efforts toward urbanization. F2-2, the development site, is co-owned by XianCun Village, a rural village that has evolved into a city district, and Poly Real Estate, one of China's top real estate developers. The two clients have agreed to jointly manage the retail and underground parking area, but desire defined and separate office towers, allowing the clients to manage, rent, and sell the office spaces independently.

The design solution situates two office towers on top of a five-story retail base. Each office tower is self-sufficient with direct street access, a lobby, and elevator banks. An interlocking L-shape configuration defines the tower spaces, situating one north–south oriented tower on the eastern edge of the site and one east–west oriented tower on the northern edge. The towers are placed above a base structure that houses retail spaces as well as an underground parking facility. The lower portion of the north–south tower cuts back to allow the lower portion of the east–west tower to extend underneath, creating a defined presence on the lot's east edge. The L-shape configuration formed by the two towers opens toward Guangzhou's central park and Pearl River, becoming an integral part of the whole spatial sequence of this "new axis" of Guangzhou. The interlocking massing also creates a strong image reflecting the cooperative relationship of the two owners, both symbolically and programmatically. The placement of the two towers also minimizes the impact from the cores to the retail base below. An open mid-block pedestrian walkway occupies the gap between the two interlocked office towers, bringing in natural light to office areas as well as pedestrian flow to support the retail shops.

In response to the hot and humid local climate, a Revit-IES study was performed to explore different skin and curtain wall strategies in terms of solar gain and daylight penetration levels. This study, though preliminary, proved to be an important first step in generating a building envelope that addresses issues of aesthetics, sustainability, and financial parameters.

Green roofs, water reuse strategies, and the possible application of wind turbines further address environmental stewardship, and rooftop gardens afford the building occupants an area of refuge from the city below.

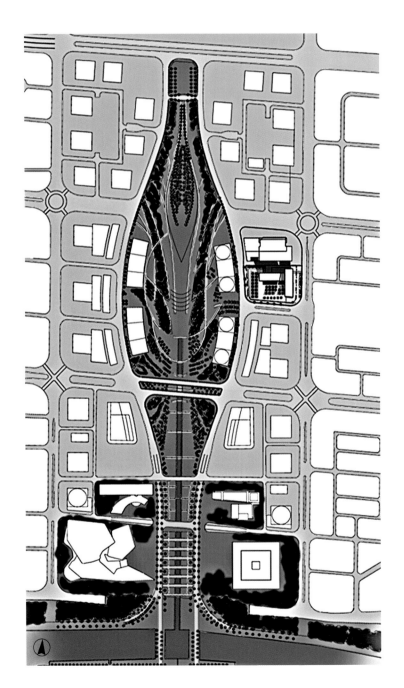

Guangzhou Pearl River Towers

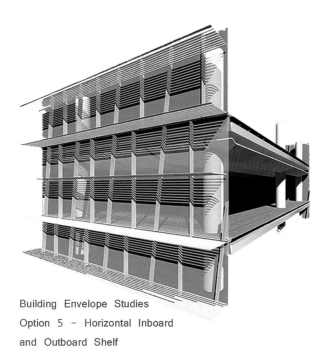

Building Envelope Studies
Option 5 – Horizontal Inboard
and Outboard Shelf

Solar Gain (Btu/h)

JAN | FEB | MAR | APR | MAY | JUN | JUL | AUG | SEP | OCT | NOV | DEC

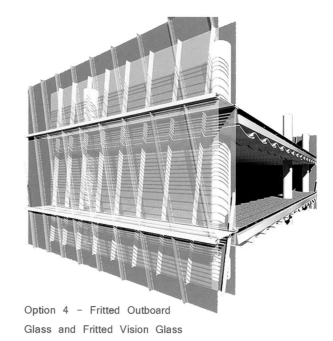

Option 4 – Fritted Outboard
Glass and Fritted Vision Glass

Solar Gain (Btu/h)

JAN | FEB | MAR | APR | MAY | JUN | JUL | AUG | SEP | OCT | NOV | DEC

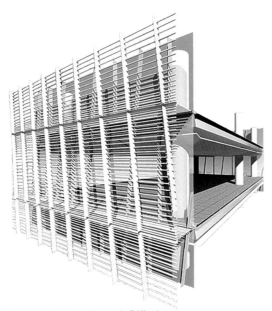

Option 3 – Horizontal Diffusing
Rods with Horizontal Shelf

Option 2 – Horizontal Diffusing
Rods

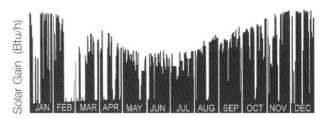

NINGBO HOTEL

DESIGN: 2007
LOCATION: NINGBO, CHINA
CLIENT: CITY OF NINGBO
AREA: 161,000 SQUARE FEET (15,000 SQUARE METERS)

A master plan has been approved for a highly active, mixed-use set of buildings on a 5-acre (2-hectare) site at the center of the Yinzhou district, within the city of Ningbo, China. At the northern edge of this area, a 161,000-square-foot (15,000-square-meter) hotel anchors the entertainment portion of the plan and presents the new development to the surrounding urban areas.

The massing is composed of a hollow cube appearing to float above a three-story plinth. The cube is clad in a pre-patinated, perforated copper outer skin that has been fractured to follow rhythms borrowed from Marcel Duchamp's *Nude Descending a Staircase*. At various intersections of the folded planes, fissures have been created to allow views through to the clear glass cube behind. The base below is enclosed by a clear and colored glass curtain wall that is highly activated by electronic signage.

The 12-story cube contains 200 hotel rooms organized around a central atrium, the surface of which is covered by angled green ceramic rods recalling the random character of a bamboo forest. The green roof-covered communal spaces below include restaurants, meeting halls, and a spa adjacent to a 100-foot-long (30-meter) swimming pool that projects through the exterior wall to form a water-filled balcony.

Two levels of below-grade parking support the programmed areas. At grade, a richly planted garden and paved walkways buffer the environment and provide connection to the riverfront, just to the west.

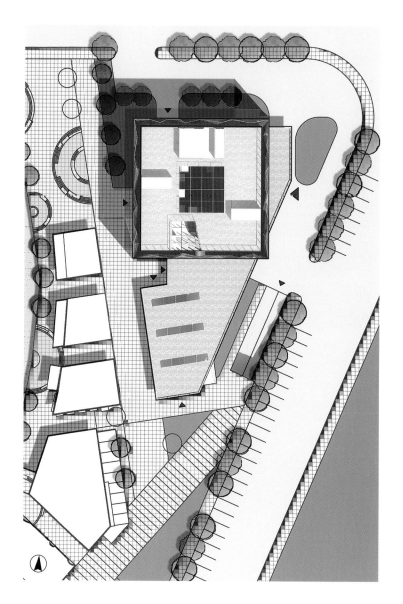

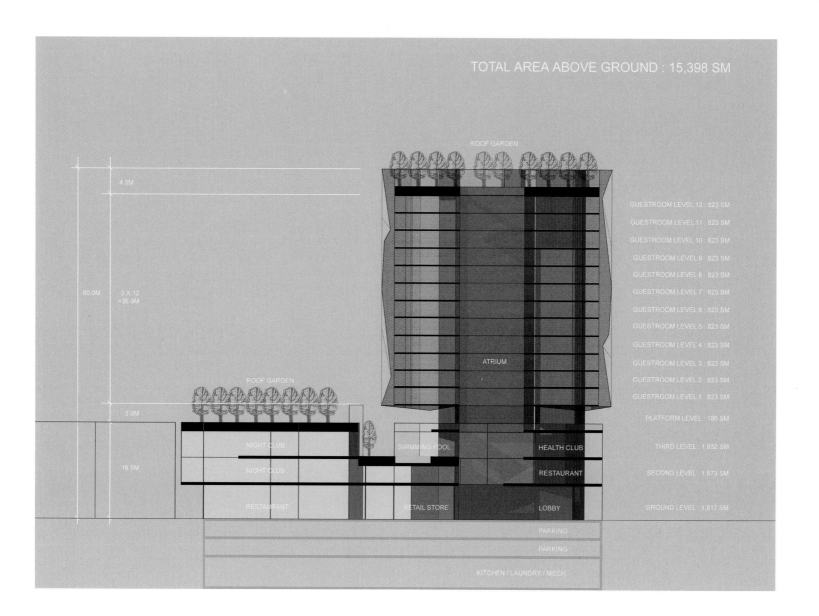

TOTAL AREA ABOVE GROUND : 15,398 SM

ROOF GARDEN

4.5M

60.0M   3 X 12
         =36.0M

GUESTROOM LEVEL 12 : 823 SM
GUESTROOM LEVEL 11 : 823 SM
GUESTROOM LEVEL 10 : 823 SM
GUESTROOM LEVEL 9 : 823 SM
GUESTROOM LEVEL 8 : 823 SM
GUESTROOM LEVEL 7 : 823 SM
GUESTROOM LEVEL 6 : 823 SM
GUESTROOM LEVEL 5 : 823 SM
GUESTROOM LEVEL 4 : 823 SM
GUESTROOM LEVEL 3 : 823 SM
GUESTROOM LEVEL 2 : 823 SM
GUESTROOM LEVEL 1 : 823 SM

ATRIUM

ROOF GARDEN

3.0M

PLATFORM LEVEL : 186 SM

NIGHT CLUB   SWIMMING POOL   HEALTH CLUB   THIRD LEVEL : 1,832 SM

16.5M   NIGHT CLUB   RESTAURANT   SECOND LEVEL : 1,873 SM

RESTAURANT   RETAIL STORE   LOBBY   GROUND LEVEL : 1,817 SM

PARKING

PARKING

KITCHEN / LAUNDRY / MECH.

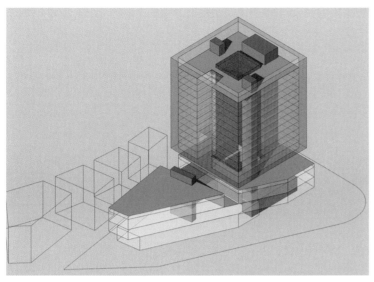
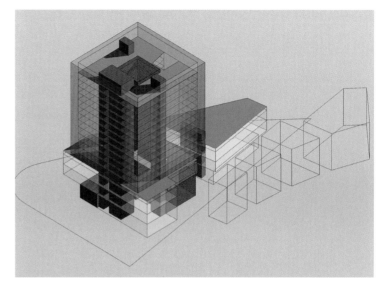
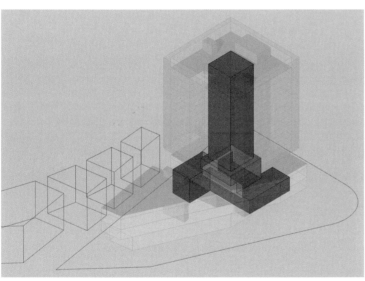
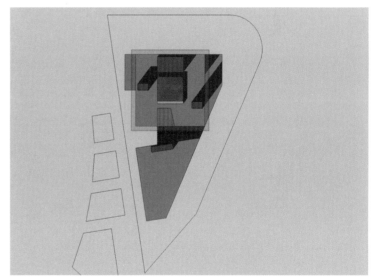

CAMPBELL SOUP COMPANY EMPLOYEE SERVICES BUILDING

DESIGN / COMPLETION: 2008 / 2009
LOCATION: CAMDEN, NEW JERSEY
CLIENT: CAMPBELL SOUP COMPANY
AREA: 100,000 SQUARE FEET ON 40 ACRES (9,300 SQUARE METERS ON 16 HECTARES)

As part of Campbell's ongoing efforts to represent innovation, progression, and a stimulation of local economic growth, it plans to construct a modern, ecologically friendly structure to house employee services and act as the new "front door" to its corporate campus. The 100,000-square-foot (9,300-square-meter) structure will highlight the world headquarters and Campbell's continued commitment to the adjacent community.

The Employee Services Building consists of three levels. The grade level houses a cafeteria, servery, kitchen, employee store, as well as the lobby and reception areas. Training facilities, conference rooms, and office space are on the upper level and connect to adjacent office zones within the neighboring buildings. A fitness center, and campus-wide printing and mail services occupy the lower level and connect to a new service area to the south.

The Employee Services Building will terminate the arrival sequence of those visiting the corporate campus. An open area that serves as the reception and an exhibition hall occupies the double-height linear atrium that is enclosed by a clear glass curtain wall. Supergraphics displaying the company logo and changing exhibitions reflecting Campbell's numerous brands project through the glass wall to welcome employees and visitors while reinforcing the rich company history. The glass curtain wall allows natural light to filter through office and work spaces that occupy both upper and lower levels.

The central location of the Employee Services Building creates an opportunity to unify the current campus by physically connecting to the other major buildings and by creating a landscaped courtyard as a shared amenity. Within this secure environment, dining and company events are planned.

Beyond the clear glass on the north façade, which cantilevers beyond the building edges to define landscaped courtyards beyond, brick is the primary exterior material. While responsive to the existing context, the masonry is detailed to be honest about its non-load-bearing capacity and is interrupted by colored glass panels that project colored sunlight into the interior and frame forever modified views of the surrounding area.

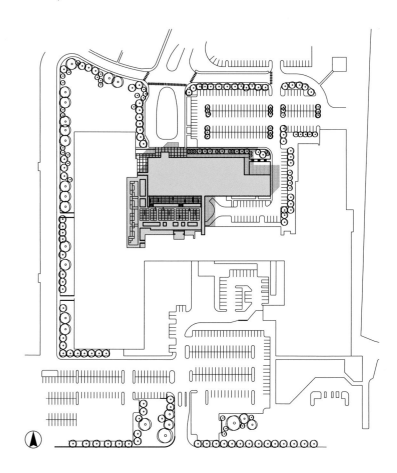

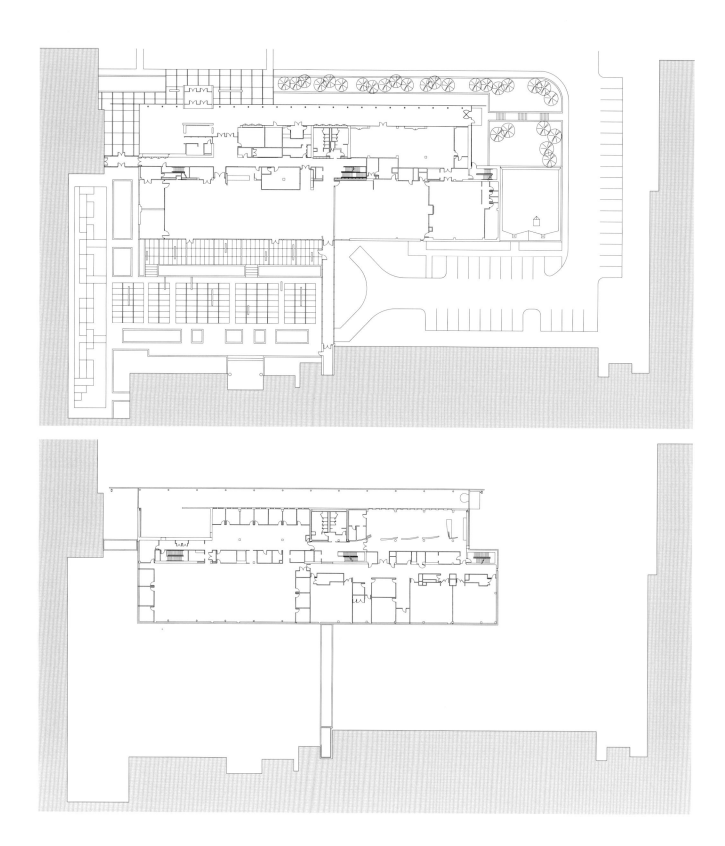

420   Campbell Soup Company Employee Services Building

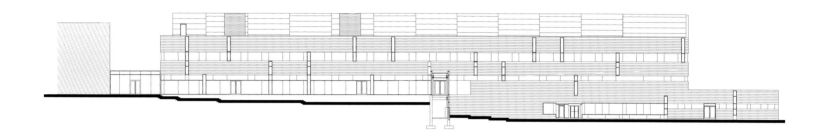

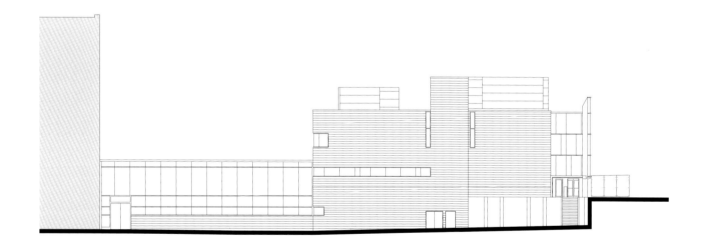

ST. LAWRENCE UNIVERSITY JOHNSON HALL OF SCIENCE

(IN ASSOCIATION WITH CROXTON COLLABORATIVE ARCHITECTS)

DESIGN / COMPLETION: 2004 / 2007
LOCATION: CANTON, NEW YORK
CLIENT: ST. LAWRENCE UNIVERSITY
AREA: 120,000 SQUARE FEET (11,100 SQUARE METERS)

St. Lawrence University, one of the nation's premier liberal arts colleges, has a keen appreciation for the importance of science education and the Johnson Hall of Science is palpable evidence of this commitment. Johnson Hall is the first entirely new teaching laboratory to be built at St. Lawrence in several decades. The program comprises 120,000 square feet (11,100 square meters) of space and includes facilities for physics, geology, mathematics and computer sciences, environmental science, and psychology.

Although the building is thoroughly modern in its program and technology, it was carefully designed to be respectful of the existing architectural character of the St. Lawrence campus. The massing, height, and materiality are designed to both blend in and stand out on campus. The materials used include a blend of Georgian brick and local stone masonry accents.

One of the key design goals for the new building was to demonstrate the viability of sustainable design principles. Hence, the new structure was very carefully sited as two parallel wings on a true north–south axis to take full advantage of daylight harvesting. There is also a high-insulation envelope roof, dimmable fluorescent lighting, intelligent occupancy sensors for the HVAC system, heat recovery for the ventilation exhaust, and high-insulation glazing. In total, the building is designed to consume approximately 30 percent less energy than a conventional design. In recognition of this innovative design and engineering approach, the US Green Building Council awarded Johnson Hall a LEED® Gold Certification.

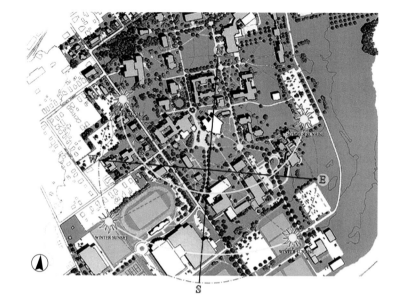

KELLOGG EYE CENTER EXPANSION AND DIABETES RESEARCH CENTER

DESIGN / COMPLETION: 2007 / 2009
LOCATION: ANN ARBOR, MICHIGAN
CLIENT: UNIVERSITY OF MICHIGAN
AREA: 222,000 SQUARE FEET (20,600 SQUARE METERS)

This project adds 222,000 square feet (20,600 square meters) of research space to the world-renowned University of Michigan Kellogg Eye Center. The addition abuts the existing facility and faces a park and the Huron River to the south as well as future university development to the north. It is a project influenced by its small site, extensive program, and proximity to existing structures. The goal was to design a 21st-century building reflecting the vision of its community of clinicians and researchers.

The massing of the Kellogg Eye Center Expansion is modulated to create a harmonious composition with the original building. The use of the center's original materials of brick, glass, and concrete has been extended, but informed by the specifics of the interior environments and with more expansive areas of clear glass.

Maximizing daylight is also a significant organizing principle of the plan. The major public components of the program including general lobby, vertical circulation, primary building circulation, and meeting areas occupy the building's perimeter, while spaces requiring progressively less light are moved further inboard.

The building features two primary open spaces. The first is the general entry that is found at levels one and two, which sets the tone for the rest of the building. This double-story space includes the reception/information desk, elevator lobbies, connection to the existing Eye Center, and views through its expansive glass wall to the future garden. The original façade and entry of the existing Center have been redesigned and expanded to create a light-filled space connecting to the original building's lobby. Daytime use of this space will include waiting, dining, and meeting by occupants from both buildings. During off hours, it has also been envisioned as a venue to host social activities. The second space is found at levels five and six where the new Brehm Center will be located. The arrival to the center occurs in a double-story space designed to function as a lobby, and also to promote creativity and collaboration. Multiple digital monitors are connected to scientists around the globe, making the Brehm Center the leading Type 1 diabetes research center in the world.

A key characteristic of the Eye Center Expansion is that it has been designed to accommodate a patient population that suffers from impaired sight or low vision. As a result, color, light, and texture are enhanced as tools to help those with vision problems navigate the clinical and surgical floors of the center.

BRANDYWINE REALTY TRUST CORPORATE HEADQUARTERS

DESIGN / COMPLETION: 2006 / 2007
LOCATION: RADNOR, PENNSYLVANIA
CLIENT: BRANDYWINE REALTY TRUST
AREA: 53,000 SQUARE FEET (4,900 SQUARE METERS)

The design of Brandywine Realty Trust's headquarters reflects the company's growth from a mature, stable organization to a cutting-edge development firm. Brandywine Realty Trust (BRT) selected space for itself that proved difficult to lease, with severely limited views and daylight on one of its two floors, thus demanding an innovative design.

In order to increase administrative efficiencies, BRT consolidated all primary corporate functions as well as regional leasing and real estate support functions into its new space. BRT's goal was to promote better communication and collaboration between corporate leadership by co-locating these functions. The aim was a workplace infused with spaces for collaboration, team-building, and creative work. Consequently, flexible teaming areas and a retooled workplace standards program were implemented to improve work processes and inter- and intra-departmental communications.

The reception space features a highly transparent entry wall and a contrasting monumental front door. Faced in acid-etched steel sheets, the large door (8 x 10 feet/2.4 x 3.1 meters) pivots to allow passage. Black quartzite stone tile, trimmed in 1/4-inch-thick (6.4-millimeter) steel banding, is used to clad one long wall and the low fireplace block. The reception floor is white terrazzo with a bamboo inset that is used to anchor the reception seating group. Anigre wood panels define the conference center beyond. A sweeping monumental staircase stands in the middle of the reception area and is constructed from painted structural steel, terrazzo treads, and glass-beaded stainless-steel guardrails. Backlit expanded metal ceiling tiles, suspended in a V-shaped frame, open views from the lobby to the new staircase.

Within office areas, workstations are planned at a slight angle to the structural grid in spaces that feature and celebrate building construction by exposing building systems including ductwork, columns, and structural elements. Private offices, faced in custom-designed glass fronts, flow seamlessly into open areas, encouraging communication at all levels of Brandywine Realty Trust's organization.

The design features a number of sustainable design strategies, including high recycled-content finishes, regional and rapidly renewable materials, and energy-efficient lighting and controls. The pre-existing shell was left in a relatively raw condition, with new materials applied as vignettes to heighten contrasts between new and old, and raw and refined. This attitude eliminated the need to re-clad and hide all existing building structure and systems, thereby reducing overall raw material usage.

SMITHSONIAN INSTITUTE FIELD RESEARCH STATIONS

DESIGN: 2007
LOCATION: REPUBLIC OF PANAMA
CLIENT: SMITHSONIAN TROPICAL RESEARCH INSTITUTION
AREA: FROM 400 SQUARE FEET (37 SQUARE METERS)

For more than 85 years, the rich ecological diversity of Panama has served as the ideal tropical research environment for biologists training with the Smithsonian Tropical Research Institution. Looking at ways to improve on-site marine and terrestrial data investigation, conceptual studies of next-generation mobile research stations were developed. These designs fuse high-technology research components into compact, yet expandable, modules that can be easily deployed to and removed from various field conditions. The simplicity and sleekness of the lightweight designs assist transportability and ease of deployment. The concepts investigate various types of modular construction including adaptive re-use of shipping containers.

By their very nature, these research stations require a certain responsibility to the environments they are investigating. The modules, in effect, should exist as self-contained organisms, cohabitating with little disruption to their surroundings; cleanliness is of major importance. Sustainable features such as photovoltaic panels and gray water collection systems are incorporated into roof configurations.

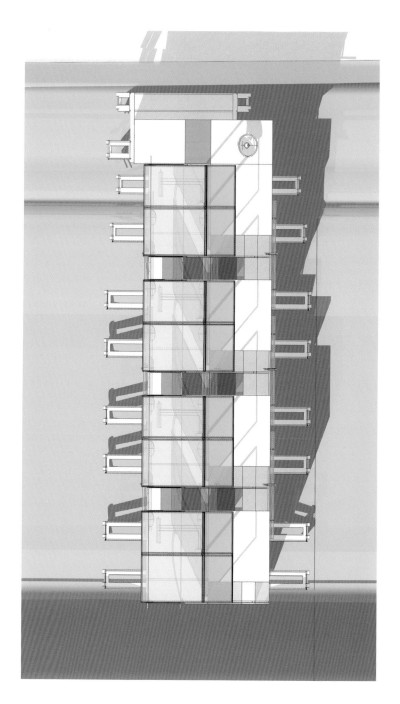

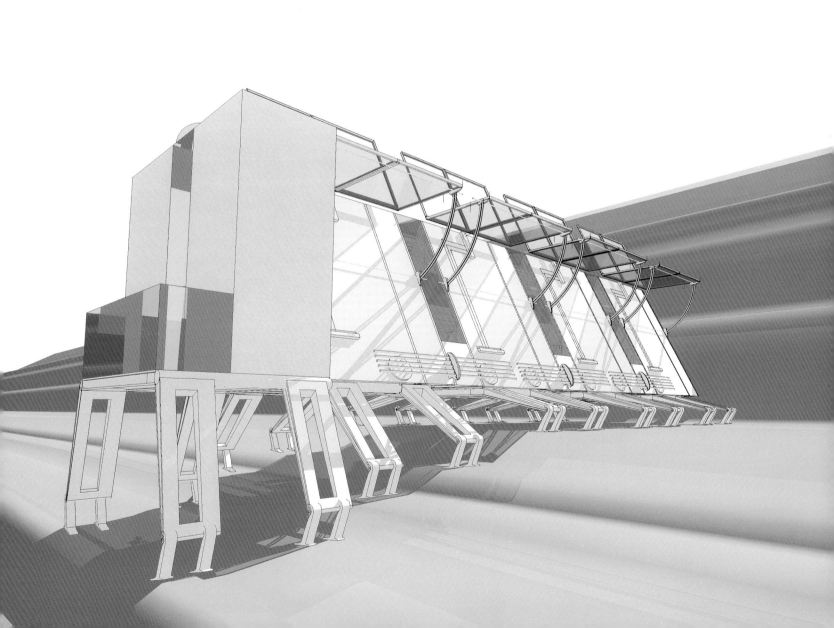

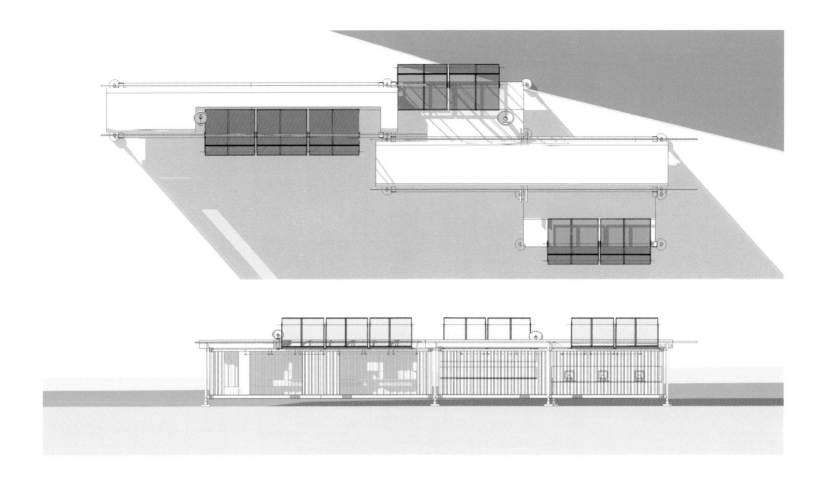

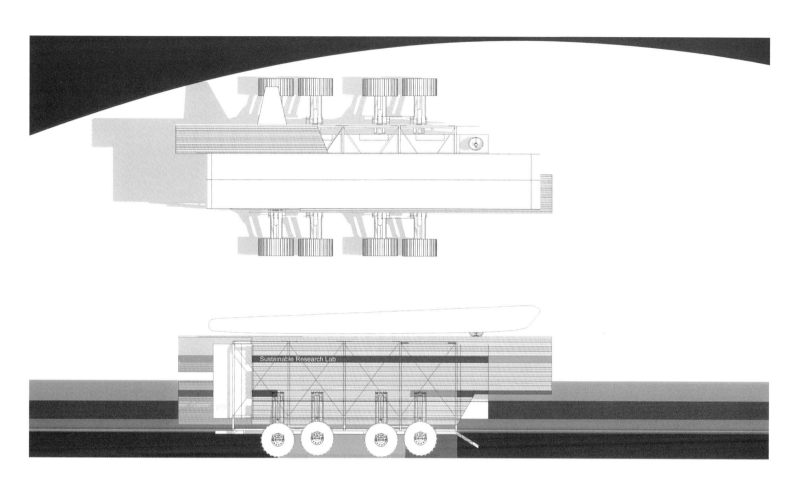

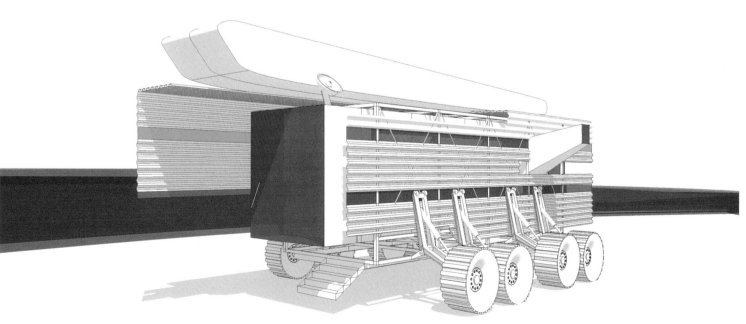

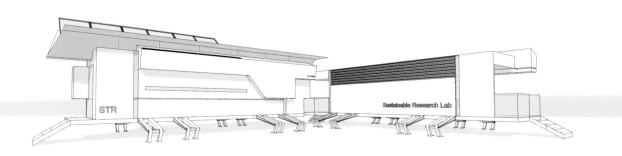

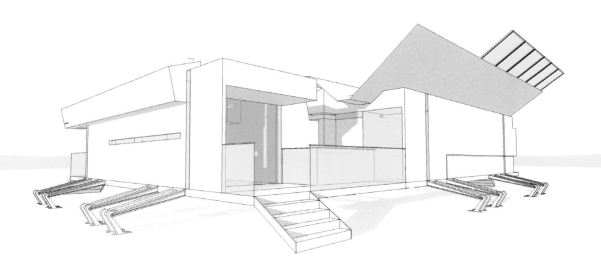

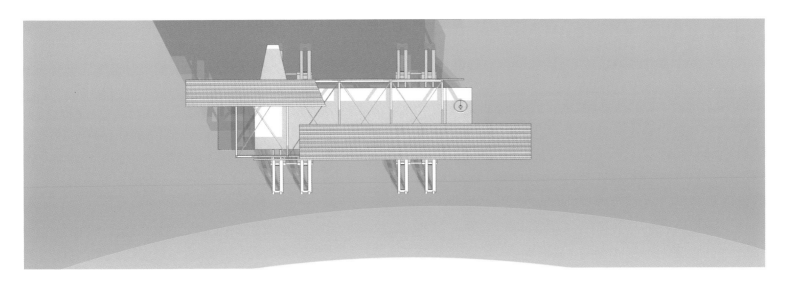

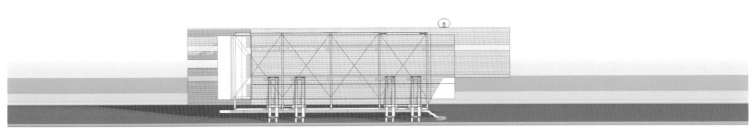

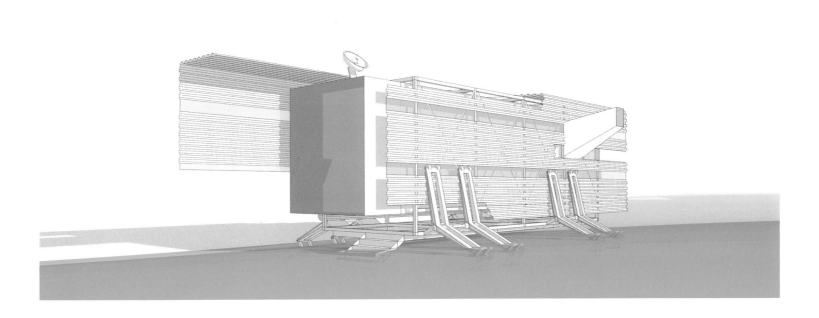

THE HILLSBOROUGH MIXED-USE TOWER

DESIGN / COMPLETION: 2008 / 2010
LOCATION: RALEIGH, NORTH CAROLINA
CLIENT: THE REYNOLDS COMPANIES
AREA: 266,000 SQUARE FEET (24,700 SQUARE METERS)

The Hillsborough is a landmark development for downtown Raleigh, North Carolina, marking the city's rapid transition from a governmental center into a dynamic urban core. The project represents a new building typology for this city and region: an integrated mixed-use program within a compact design on a small site that offers guests and residents a high level of amenity, service, and sophistication.

Located at a highly visible site in the heart of downtown, two blocks from the North Carolina state capitol, The Hillsborough will establish a new benchmark for architectural design, luxury hotel accommodation, and urban dwelling in Raleigh. This project will create the first five-star hotel in Raleigh, with amenities that include a rooftop swimming pool, a full-service ballroom, and meeting rooms. The building's residents will also have full access to all of the hotel facilities, creating a unique opportunity for an urban lifestyle that cannot be found elsewhere in the region.

The design objective is to create an iconic building that promotes pedestrian activity at street level while simultaneously making a significant contribution to the Raleigh skyline. The entire ground floor of the project, including three street frontages and the parking structure, is dedicated to building lobby, restaurant, and retail uses. The building massing and the exterior character each expresses the functional organization of the building while creating an articulation of the building mass that is sympathetic with its predominantly small-scale context. A screen of precast concrete defines the 12-story hotel with large-scale openings corresponding to the guest rooms behind, while the residential tower is clad with a transparent curtain wall, providing unobstructed views from the dwellings and engaging in a continuous dialogue with both the sky and skyline. These distinct elements are unified as a series of overlapping planes, creating a dynamic expression for the building exterior that asserts its presence with confidence and respect to its surroundings.

NATIONAL GEOSPATIAL-INTELLIGENCE AGENCY NEW CAMPUS EAST

DESIGN / COMPLETION: 2009 / 2011
LOCATION: FORT BELVOIR, VIRGINIA
CLIENT: U.S. ARMY CORPS OF ENGINEERS, BALTIMORE DISTRICT
AREA: 2,400,000 SQUARE FEET (223,000 SQUARE METERS)

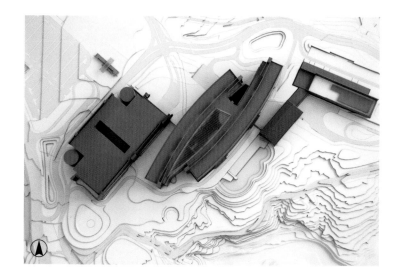

KlingStubbins, in a joint venture with RTKL, is working with the US Army Corps of Engineers, Baltimore to deliver a master plan, full A/E/I design services, as well as site, civil, and landscape design for a new large-scale, secure government headquarters campus for the National Geospatial-Intelligence Agency (NGA). The campus will consolidate 8,500 employees on approximately 130 acres (53 hectares) of the Engineering Proving Grounds at Fort Belvoir, Virginia as part of the Base Realignment and Closure Act. This environmentally sensitive site is adjacent to the Accotink Creek.

The 2,400,000-square-foot (223,000-square-meter) campus will house secure and redundant services for multiple buildings and support facilities, including: a visitor control center; remote delivery facility; technology center; central utility plant; and a main administrative/office building housing operations facilities, conference and training functions, auditorium, multiple food service venues, fitness center, and library. The campus is being designed to accommodate 5,100 cars in structured parking.

A primary objective of the new campus design is to reinforce and enhance NGA's operational goal to utilize the consolidation as a vehicle to achieve cultural transformation. The design team worked closely with NGA to understand and identify the primary organizational and cultural attributes to be reflected in the building design. The resultant design concept creates an environment that reinforces collaboration and a single community identity.

The new campus is being designed and built through multiple phases. It is being designed to meet LEED® Silver Certification with the US Green Building Council, furthering environmental stewardship on behalf of the US government, ensuring the use of recovered and recycled materials and efficiency in resource and material utilization. This project is currently one of the largest projects in the United States utilizing Building Information Modeling (BIM) documentation standards.

National Geospatial-Intelligence Agency New Campus East

CASTLEWAY MIXED-USE DEVELOPMENT

DESIGN: 2008
LOCATION: PHILADELPHIA, PENNSYLVANIA
CLIENT: CASTLEWAY PROPERTIES, LLC
AREA: 575,000 SQUARE FEET (53,400 SQUARE METERS)

At the northwest corner of Rittenhouse Square, Philadelphia's premier residential address, a long vacant lot is being master planned to accommodate a high-end condominium, a luxury hotel, and extensive ground-floor retail. A 40-foot-wide (12-meter) park defines the eastern edge and provides a pedestrian link between Walnut and Sansom Streets.

Programmatically the complex will contain 150 condominiums, 200 hotel rooms, restaurants, a spa, and a rooftop pool. Green roofs provide both visual and ecological benefit, and help integrate the towers with Rittenhouse Square and the newly created park.

The 575,000-square-foot (53,400-square-meter) complex includes a thin condominium tower composed of two narrow parallel plates on the north edge, and a perpendicular intersecting hotel slab. The south face of the hotel defines the edge of the Square and is directly responsive to the scale of neighboring buildings. The residential tower's height of 525 feet (160 meters) is sympathetic to the urban fabric just to the north. The first floor of both buildings is almost entirely clear glass to infuse the streetscape with activity.

The buildings' character is most determined by the highly mutable qualities of clear glass with transparency and reflectivity constantly changing one's awareness. External solar screens and silk-screened and colored glass provide complexity and depth, and mitigate issues of heat gain. Verdigris copper bars and perforated panels shelter the hotel walls and building base.

Below-grade parking and servicing, three frontages of retail, and the newly created park/mews afford the community a vibrant addition to the city. It is envisioned that the development will instigate a regeneration of the northwest corner of the Square and, in doing so, promote revitalization north to Chestnut Street and west to the Schuylkill River. The intention to achieve a minimum of LEED® Gold Certification further enhances the development's benefits.

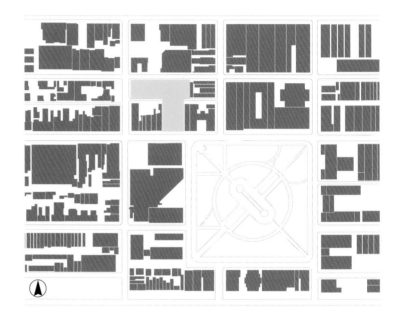

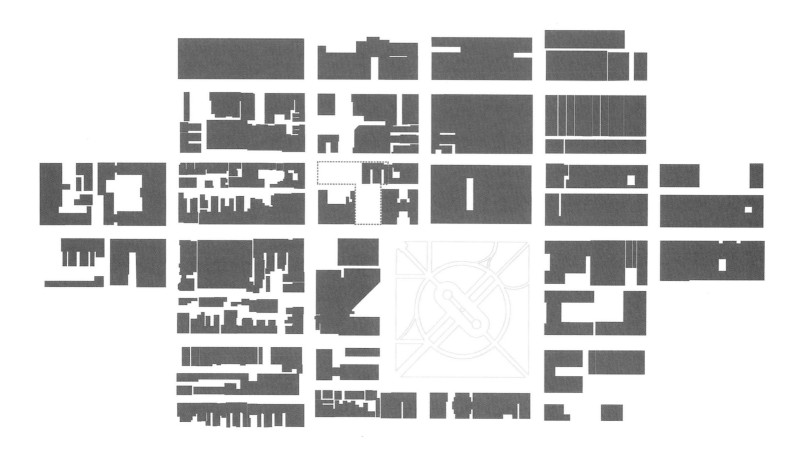

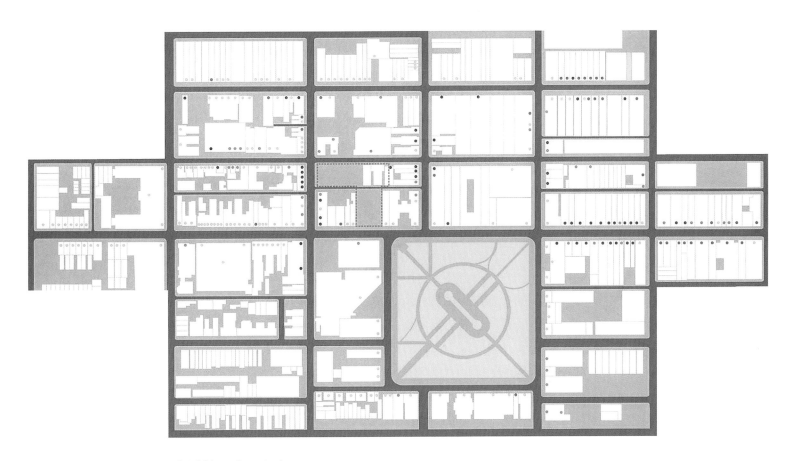

- Retail (shops & services)
- Restaurant
- Residential
- Hospitality
- Office
- Cultural/religious
- Bank
- Garage

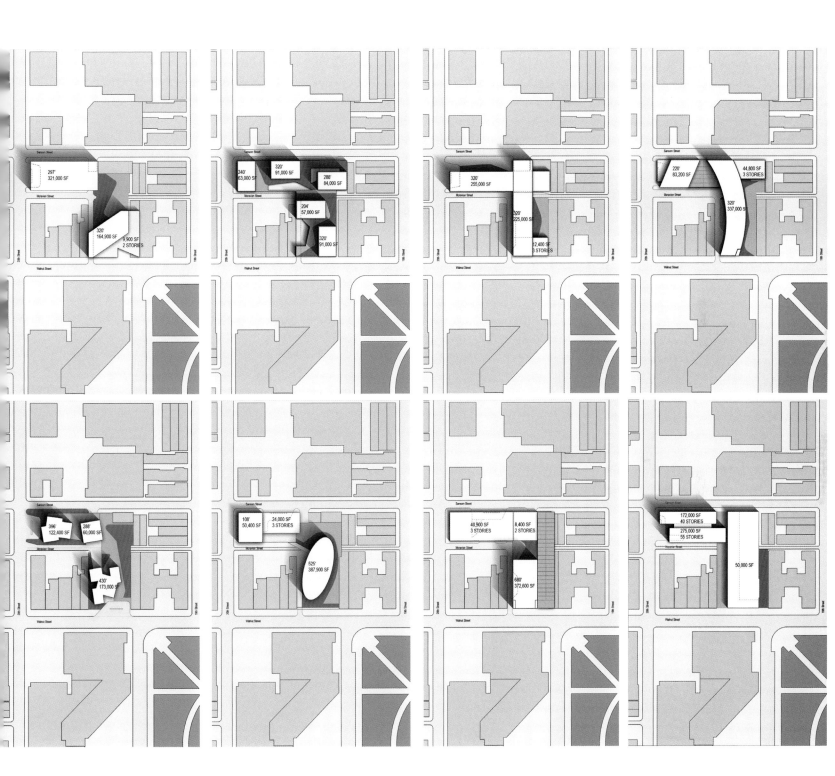

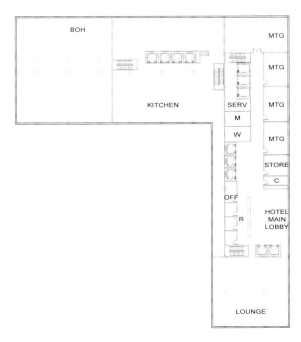

3rd floor: 25,889 GSF

33rd – 42nd:
10 x 6,775 = 67,750 GSF

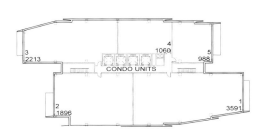

19th – 32nd:
14 x 10,901 = 152,614 GSF

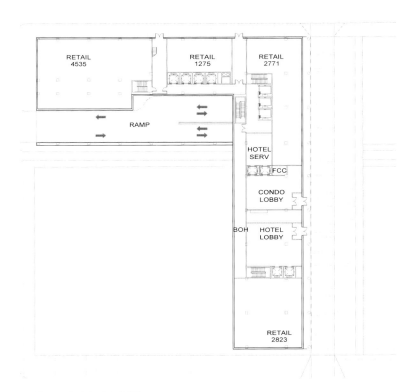

Ground: 24,500 GSF

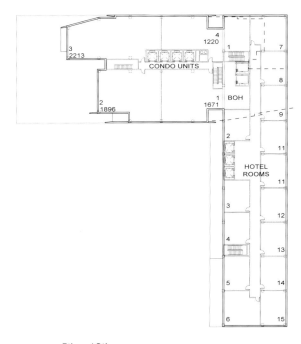

5th – 18th:
12 x 19,642 = 235,704 GSF

Castleway Mixed-Use Development

GATEWAY CENTER AT SONGDO CITY

DESIGN: 2007
LOCATION: INCHEON, SOUTH KOREA
CLIENT: GALE INTERNATIONAL
AREA: 3,500,000 SQUARE FEET (325,000 SQUARE METERS)

The proposed design for the Gateway Center places five office towers atop a three-story retail base and an underground parking facility. Towers B, C, and D are situated to define the street edge along Park Avenue, while Towers A and E form a counter geometry reflective of the street grid to the east. Stretched between these two buildings is an urban plaza that connects the entire Center.

Tower A on block F6-2 is the most significant of the five towers. It forms a figural gateway into the city and is the tallest building of the complex. The top 59 feet (18 meters) house a roof garden, offering the building occupants refuge from the city below.

Towers B and C are linked by a shared retail base with an atrium at the center that provides a public front door to the complex. Infused with natural light and enlivened by the surrounding retail shops, this environment affords a pedestrian connection between Park Avenue and the Gateway Center Plaza and begins the transition from the activity of the city streetscape to the relative calm of the plaza.

Located at the northern edge of the Gateway Center, both Towers D and E offer more singular presence and are envisioned as potentially desirable locations for corporate headquarters. With the exception of Tower A, all the other buildings comply with the "sky plane" master plan concept.

The overall impression of the Gateway Center recalls the imagery of mountains that dominate the natural landscape and heavily influence the culture of Koreans. The design is deliberately complex to convey verticality in spite of the height guidelines called for in the master plan. The massing of each building is rendered as if composed of bundles of more slender elements, resembling Brancusi's Infinite Column. The five towers together form a metaphorical mountain range, with sloping trapezoidal walls rendered in glass that alternately reflect the sky above and the city below.

The floor plans of the towers are influenced by the vernacular design of Korea. The plan figuration recalls the pattern often seen on traditional screen doors.

The Gateway Center will create a unique and vibrant complex that synthesizes Korean aesthetics with modern architecture, while respecting the guidelines of the master plan and the evolving context of this new city.

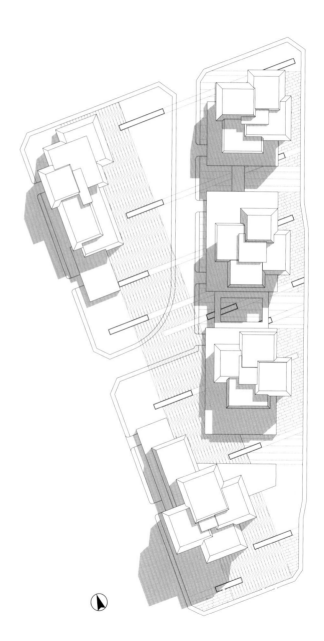

474   Gateway Center at Songdo City

　　　Gateway Center at Songdo City

Gateway Center at Songdo City

Gateway Center at Songdo City   481

DAMAC HEADQUARTERS TOWER

DESIGN / COMPLETION: 2008 /
LOCATION: DUBAI, UNITED ARAB EMIRATES
CLIENT: DAMAC HOLDING
AREA: 700,000 SQUARE FEET (65,000 SQUARE METERS)

Damac Holding, as part of its rapid expansion and growth in the region, has decided to build its headquarters building in Dubai and aims to do so with serious consideration to the character and influence of architecture. Aspiring to create a landmark building that can reflect Damac's vision, the firm has requested a design that is not simply another outlandish, structurally challenged form, but a simple representation of corporate prowess expressed in a refined architectural vocabulary.

The tower is to be 50 to 55 stories above a five-story retail and parking base, with a tower footprint of approximately 10,700 square feet (1,000 square meters). Three levels of below-grade parking and the majority of the area within the plinth are to be utilized to accommodate the zoning requirement of 1,655 cars. The roof of the plinth is envisioned as an outdoor garden and area of congregation that will be shared with a marketing center that will showcase Damac's numerous residential and commercial offerings. The tower is to be equally divided between tenant spaces on the lower half and Damac's offices above, and is to programmatically culminate in a chairman's suite that includes a garden and infinity pool.

After a concerted and broad investigation, two alternate schemes were proposed, each attempting to balance issues of views, daylighting, column-free space, and iconic character. Both address pedestrian perception and cityscape imagery.

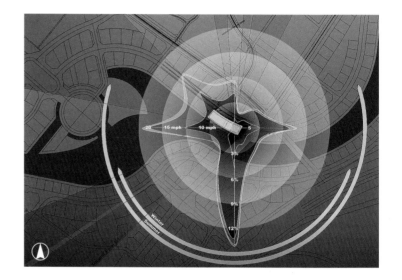

The slab scheme is predicated on true north–south orientation, a clear span 33-foot (10-meter) lease depth, and maximizing views to the Burj Dubai directly to the north. Clad in floor-to-ceiling glass and offering panoramic views from every level, the building offers a transparent and luminous icon to the skyline. The PVC-clad elliptical marketing center hovering above the base presents a responsible representation of Dubai's new commitment to sustainability.

The box attempts to clearly address the consideration of maximizing daylight while mitigating heat gain and glare. The exterior modulates solid and void in response to solar orientation, and the central atrium provides diffused light to the office environment. Each of the spiraling erosions enhances this opportunity for daylight while simultaneously offering terraces focused on differing distant views.

Consideration for sustainability has directed much of our investigation. Triple-glazed curtain walls with integral blinds, photovoltaic cells, passive shading, wind turbines, gray water collection and reuse, under-floor air distribution coupled with chilled beam technology, and, above all else, a consideration for minimizing water usage have been integrated into the design aesthetic and realization.

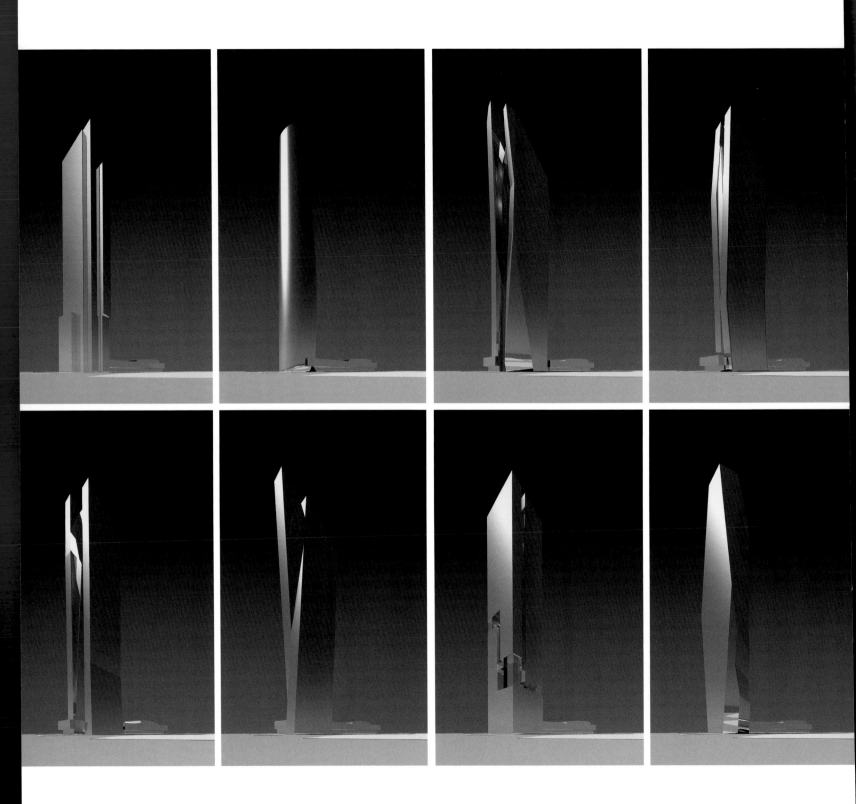

Damac Headquarters Tower

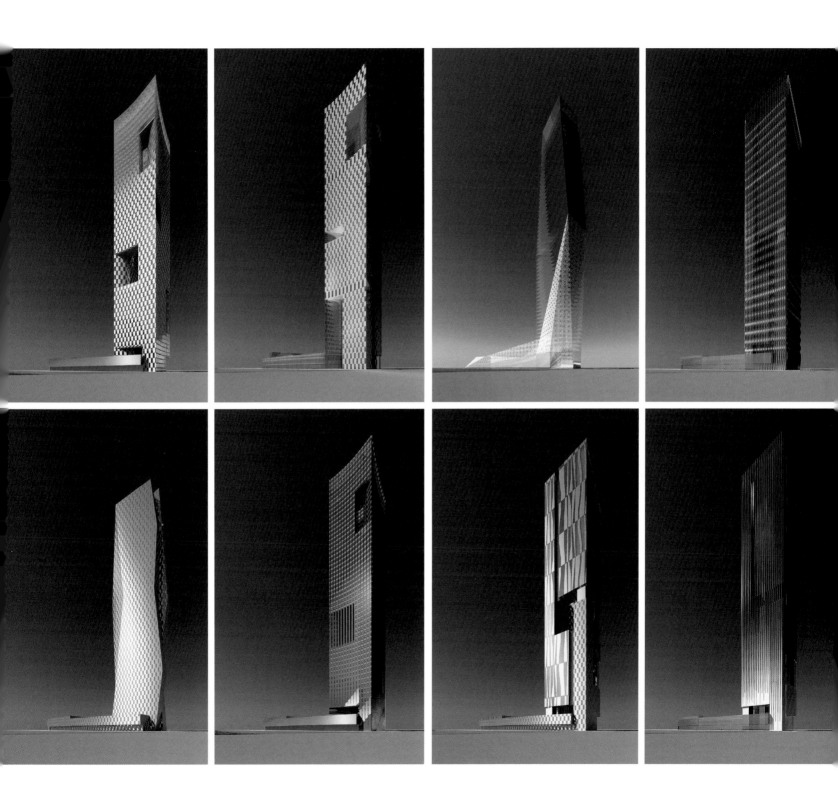

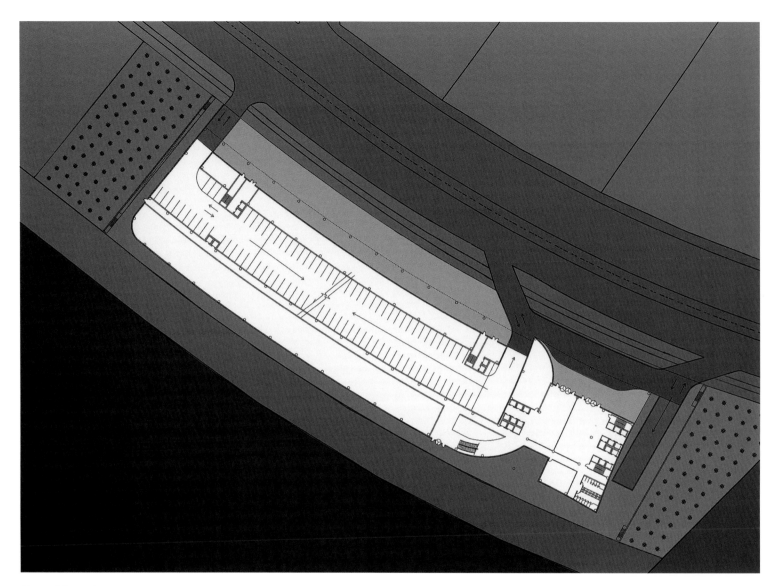

Ground floor plan

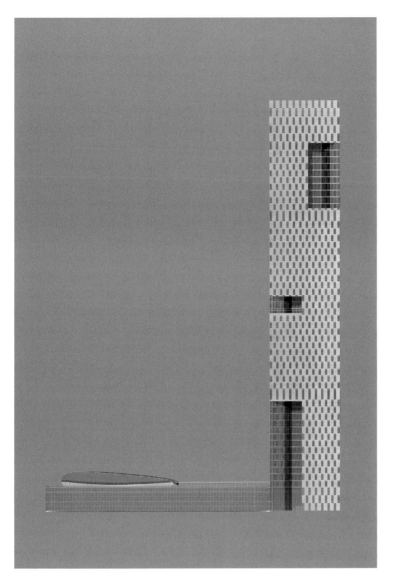
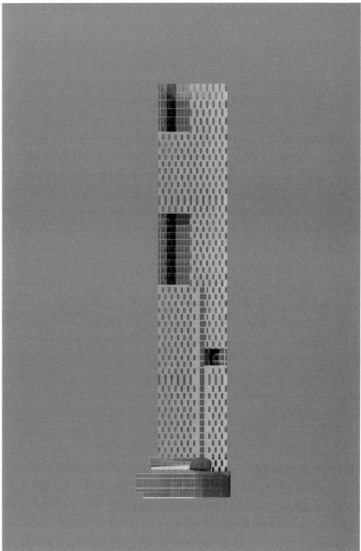

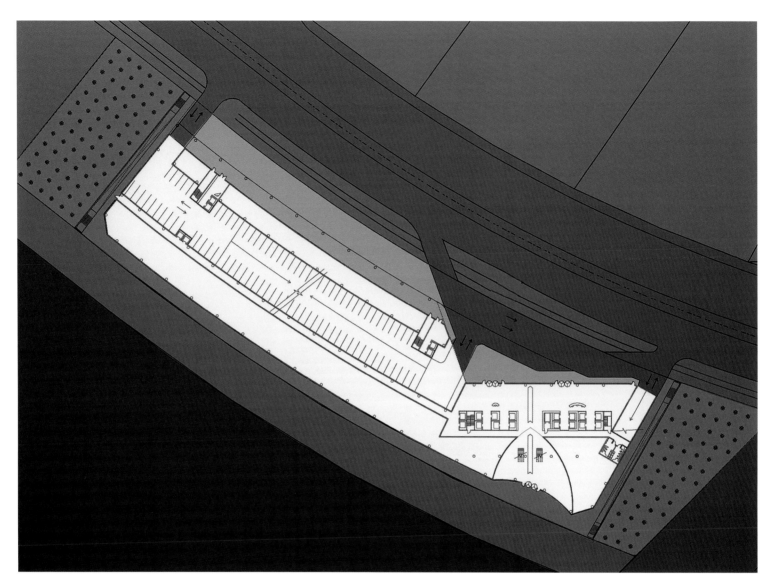

Ground floor plan

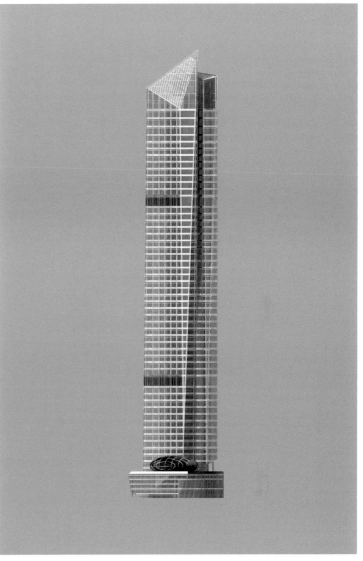

494   Damac Headquarters Tower

CITY OF WUHAN GEZHOUBA INTERNATIONAL PLAZA

DESIGN: 2008
LOCATION: WUHAN, CHINA
CLIENT: HUBEI GEZHOUBA HAIJI REAL ESTATE DEVELOPMENT LTD.
AREA: 2,600,000 SQUARE FEET (242,000 SQUARE METERS)

Seated at the strategic axis of central China's commercial mobilization, the Gezhouba International Plaza embodies iconic prominence within the fabric of Wuhan's new Central Business District. The plaza site is composed of a faceted, crystalline, 69-floor high-rise office tower to the northwest, a 34-floor condominium and hotel tower to the southeast, and connecting the two, a low-rise commercial and retail venue surrounded by a public landscape. The complex represents a new generation of super high-rises that both embrace and engage their surrounding environments. In the same way that natural structures and organisms can adapt to conditions by the most efficient means necessary, the organic geometries of the towers and the building systems employ local resources for the comfort and welfare of their occupants, enhancing function and minimizing waste. The slender mass of the office tower ensures the delivery of natural light throughout the structure. A breathing exterior envelope enables the building's state of equilibrium. The organizing principle of water, a gesture to the Yangtze River and many other waterways of the region, serves as an aesthetic catalyst for space and form, as well as a conservation method for energy systems. The design also utilizes gray water collection and wind power generation, further demonstrating its likeness to a living organism integrated into the life cycle of its environment.

Circulation and scale were primary considerations in both the plaza and plinth design. The six-story retail base is connected to the office tower via a lower-level concourse and skybridges at upper levels, crisscrossing a multi-story, skylit atrium. An anchor department store, five floors of restaurants, and other retail venues occupy the majority of this environment while sharing the top floor with a corporate auditorium and meeting rooms.

Perched atop the plinth is a succession of roof gardens, resembling agricultural terracing in abstract form. The green rooftop employs gathering spaces of different scales and materials including water gardens, field crops, large plants, and areas of paving—an ever-changing environment as one ascends from the "low lands" to the "high peaks" of the rooftop. The garden's central element, the skylit atrium, acts as a symbol of Wuhan's primary river as it winds through China's natural habitats, cultivated fields, and urban centers, and visually combines this area of respite with the endless activity below.

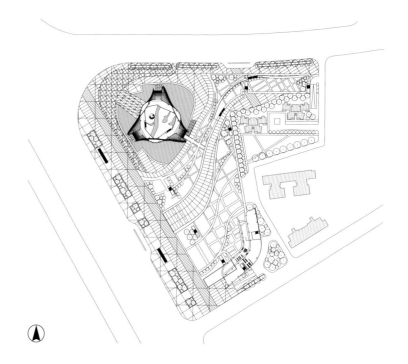

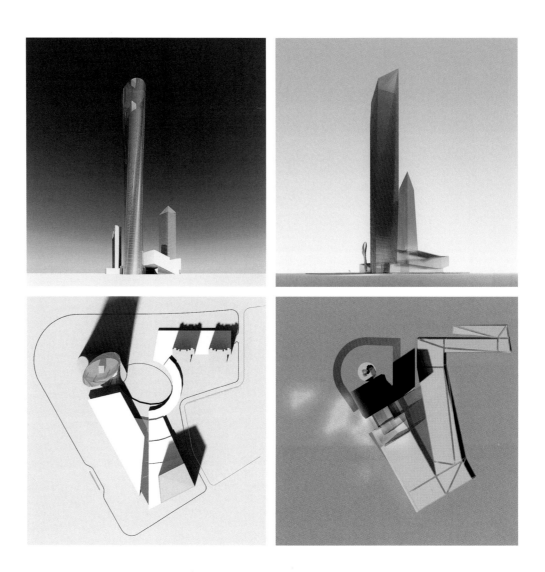

502   City of Wuhan Gezhouba International Plaza

City of Wuhan Gezhouba International Plaza

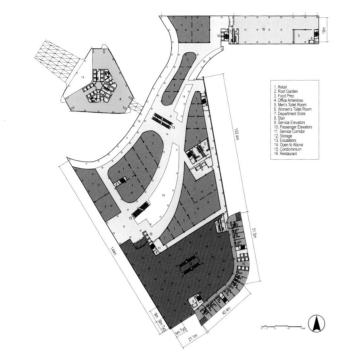

1. Retail
2. Roof Garden
3. Food Prep
4. Office Amenities
5. Men's Toilet Room
6. Women's Toilet Room
7. Department Store
8. Stair
9. Service Elevators
10. Passenger Elevators
11. Service Corridor
12. Storage
13. Escalators
14. Open to Above
15. Condominium
16. Restaurant

2nd level plan

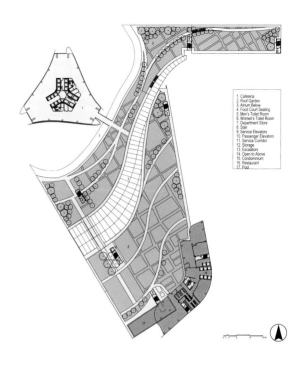

1. Cafeteria
2. Roof Garden
3. Atrium Below
4. Food Court Seating
5. Men's Toilet Room
6. Women's Toilet Room
7. Department Store
8. Stair
9. Service Elevators
10. Passenger Elevators
11. Service Corridor
12. Storage
13. Escalators
14. Open to Above
15. Condominium
16. Restaurant
17. Pool

8th level tower plan
6th level roof plan

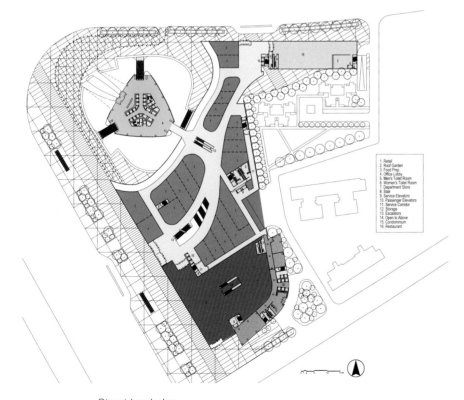

1. Retail
2. Roof Garden
3. Food Prep
4. Office Lobby
5. Men's Toilet Room
6. Women's Toilet Room
7. Department Store
8. Stair
9. Service Elevators
10. Passenger Elevators
11. Service Corridor
12. Storage
13. Escalators
14. Open to Above
15. Condominium
16. Restaurant

Street level plan

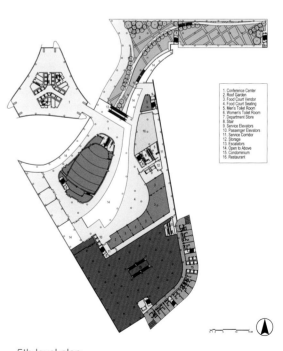

1. Conference Center
2. Roof Garden
3. Food Court Vendor
4. Food Court Seating
5. Men's Toilet Room
6. Women's Toilet Room
7. Department Store
8. Stair
9. Service Elevators
10. Passenger Elevators
11. Service Corridor
12. Storage
13. Escalators
14. Open to Above
15. Condominium
16. Restaurant

5th level plan

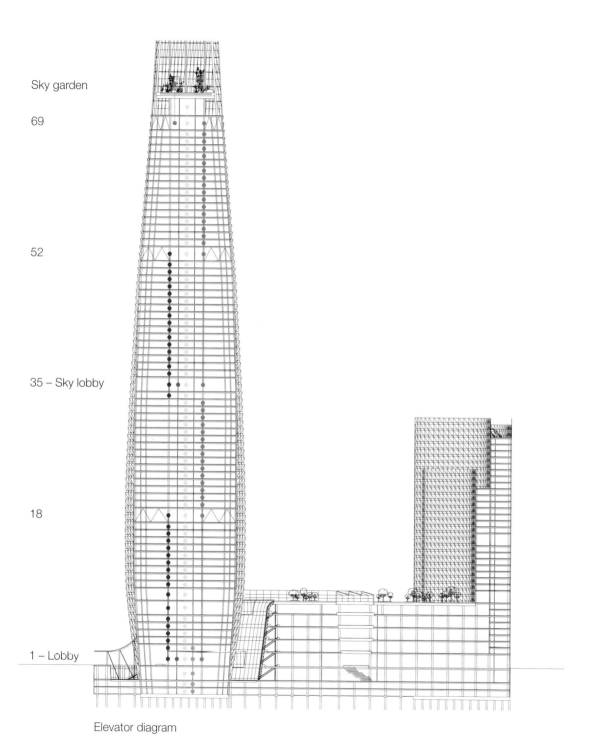

Sky garden

69

52

35 – Sky lobby

18

1 – Lobby

Elevator diagram

69th level plan

50th level plan

35th level plan

2nd level plan

Street level plan

Parking level 1 plan

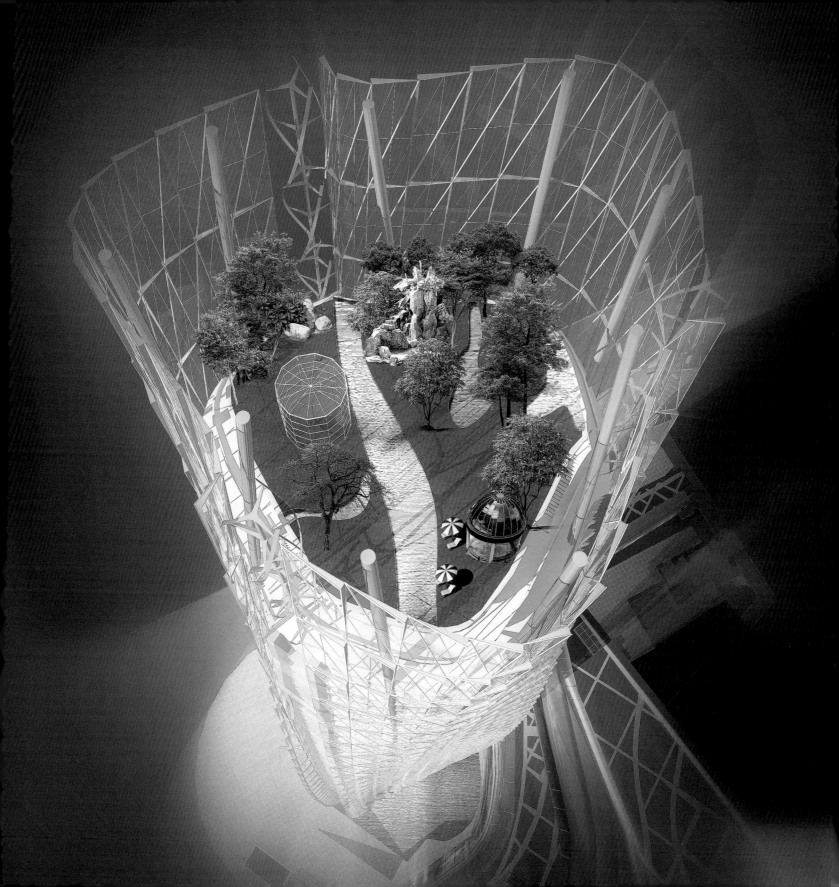

510   City of Wuhan Gezhouba International Plaza

Natural selection in the organic world ensures that healthy organisms survive by efficient use of external resources. Before the advent of mechanical conditioning systems, buildings had to work the same way— capturing prevailing breezes, shading from sun and rain, and staying warm and cool in extreme temperatures. In today's world, technology has made it possible to condition buildings beyond the passive systems of the past, but by incorporating the principles of natural selection, we can reduce the energy and resources needed to make these spaces inhabitable.

The buildings and their technical systems have been designed simultaneously in an integrated architecture/engineering process that included the following steps: analysis of weather, geology, water table, renewable energy resources; simulations and computer modeling, and evaluation of the data generated; and integration of architectural design issues with engineering criteria and strategies.

As a result of this integrated design process, eight specific technological strategies have been incorporated:

High-Performance Envelope: either a ventilated, double-skin-glazed enclosure, or a triple-glazed single skin with integral solar shades.

Under-Floor Air Distribution and Passive Chilled Beams: water as a heat transfer medium is approximately 3,500 times more efficient by volume than air.

Daylight Harvesting: the form of the towers permits all of the occupied spaces to be proximal to the exterior wall.

Solar Thermal Domestic Hot Water Production: by using rooftop areas and spandrel zones at the mechanical floors of the south face of the tower, a significant portion of hot water can be generated from solar-powered evacuated tube collectors.

Geothermal Heat Rejection: a closed loop heat exchange with the constant 20-degree Celsius groundwater will reject heat from the building's cooling plant.

Cogeneration: by locating power-generating turbines at the building site, transmission losses can be minimized.

Gray Water Collection: by collecting the site stormwater, as well as the condensate from the coils in the cooling plant, much of the nonpotable water needs can be satisfied.

Wind Power Generation: vertical wind turbines at the top of the building will contribute to the reduction of electrical power generation.

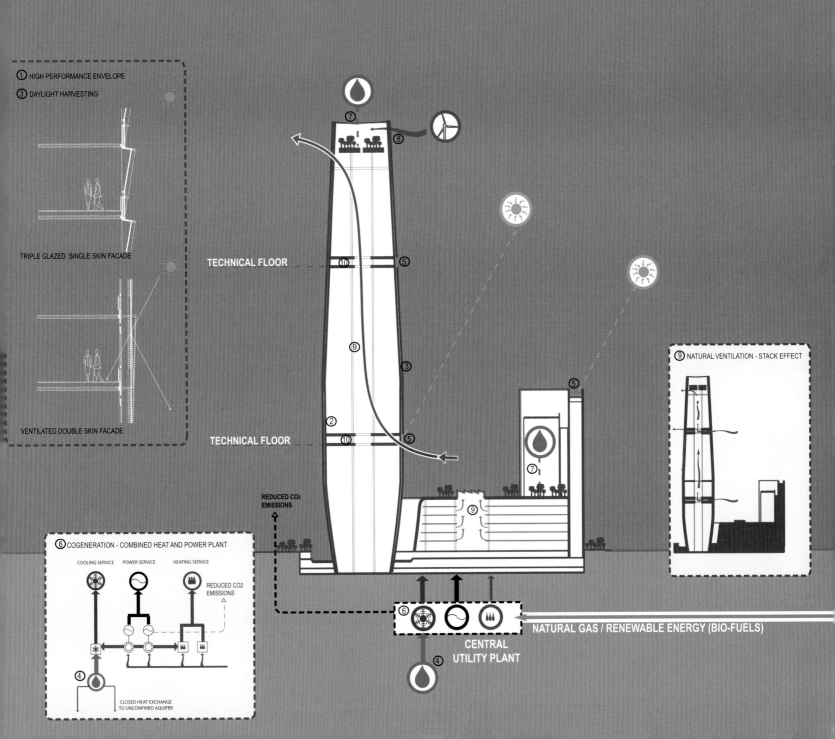

① HIGH PERFORMANCE ENVELOPE

③ DAYLIGHT HARVESTING

TRIPLE GLAZED SINGLE SKIN FACADE

VENTILATED DOUBLE SKIN FACADE

TECHNICAL FLOOR

TECHNICAL FLOOR

⑦

⑧

⑩   ⑤

③

⑨

②

⑩   ⑤

⑤

⑦

⑨

REDUCED CO2
EMISSIONS

⑨ NATURAL VENTILATION - STACK EFFECT

⑥ COGENERATION - COMBINED HEAT AND POWER PLANT

COOLING SERVICE   POWER SERVICE   HEATING SERVICE

REDUCED CO2
EMISSIONS

④

CLOSED HEAT EXCHANGE
TO UNCONFINED AQUIFER

⑥

④

CENTRAL
UTILITY PLANT

NATURAL GAS / RENEWABLE ENERGY (BIO-FUELS)

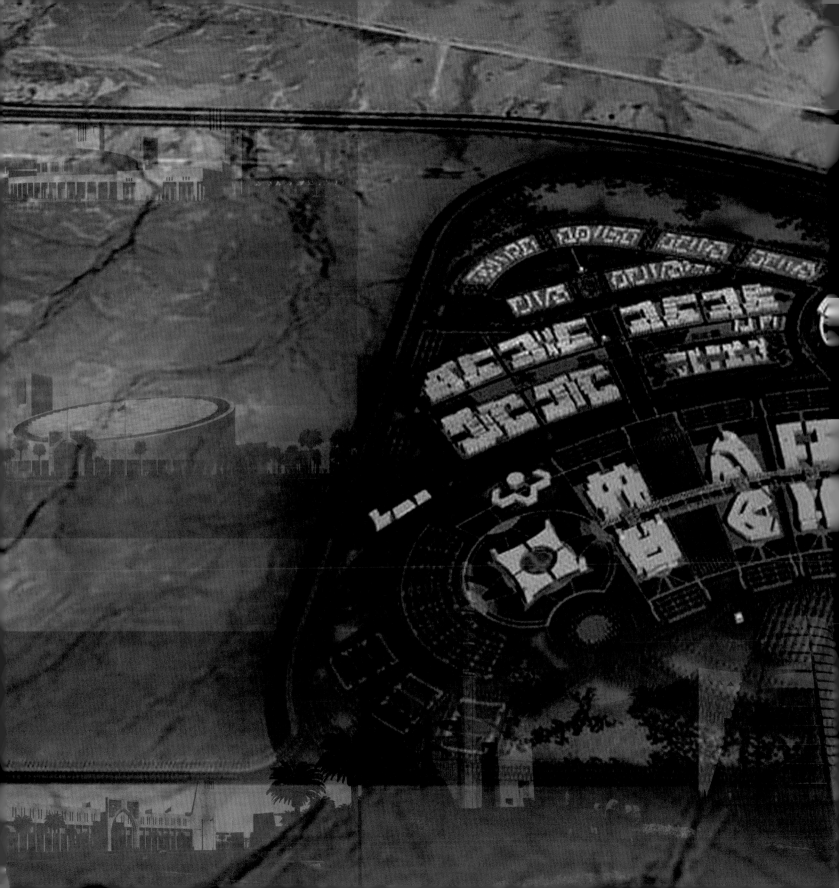

PEOPLE

Vincent G. Kling   Hugh A. Stubbins   Bradford White Fiske   Robert T. Hsu   Michael R. Lorenz   Robert G. Thompson   Peter Blewett
William Brader   Joseph Castner   Marc Clair   Jeffrey Cosiol   Leonardo Diaz   Williston Dye   Noel Fagerlund   Richard J. Farley   Richard J. Green
W. Easley Hamner   Stephen Kennerly   Richard Kirkpatrick   Helmut Krohnemann   John LaProcido   Paul Leonard   James Lindquist
Robert G. Little, Jr.   William McGee   Gerard Murray   John Neilson   C. Ronald Ostberg   Thomas E. Reed   John Robinson
Richard Rowe   Charles Rowland   Philip Seibert   Scott Simpson   Alan M. Sloan   Michael Stevenson   Kimberly R. Williams   David Altenhofen
Louis Angelus   Richard Ashworth   James Beyer   Douglas Bradley   Mark Caraccia   Alberto Cavallero   Richard Cianfrini   Joseph Cuilla   Lida
Dersookian   Raymond Doyle   Lorraine Fisher   Michael Giardina   William Gillespie   Howard Goldstein   Jeffrey Heiken   Tejoon Jung
Robert Kennedy   Michael J. Kraus   Frank Klusek   Michael Koluch   Christopher Leary   Mark Maguire   Richard Mark   Glenn Matsumoto
Patrick McGranaghan   Frank Nemia   Audrey O'Hagan   Roy Pederson   John J. Philomena   Pascal D. Pittman   Donald Posson
Srinivas Sagaram   Kenneth Schotsch   Peter Scott   Sarah Springer   John Suter   Joseph Tinari   William Vinyard   Martin Wendel
James Yadavaia   Mark Zwagerman   Debra Aungst   Judy A. Bennett   Taylor Boyd   John Brockwell   Dennis Brooks   Richard Cheetham
Scott Daniels   Scott Davis   Mary Beth Di Figlia   Diane Evans   Steven J. Gerber   Michael Gilligan   Jonathan D. Ginnis   Adam Glaser
Charles A. Hayter   James Hiser   Eric Hollenberg   Sue Hu   Mary Killough   John Kostyo   Kenneth Kutsmeda   Todd Lambert
Paul Marchese   Jeff Millett   Karen Modzelewski   Stephen Mullen   William E. Ralston   Alberto Rios   Jeffrey Salocks   Nancy Siefert
Ellen Sisle   John Stevermer   Daniel Thomas   John Trosino   W. Howard Truelove   John Turner   Jonathan Weiss   Pamela Assenmacher
Contance Ballard   Paul Bearn   Terry Bell   Linda Binstead   Kevin Blankenship   Fred Block   William Boral   Greg Bordynowski   Robert Butler
David Carlson   Elizabeth Chodosh   Frank Cheng   Stacie Ciancarelli   Nancy Darr   Thomas Dearing   Robert DeFeo   Joseph Diviney
David Doelp   John Dolph   Mac Dolton   Jack Donahue   Stephen Drobish   Mark Duckett   Ken Dubois   Mark Farmer   Stephen Favieri
Joseph Fazio   Marc Fischer   Allen Frakes   Marcelo Franganillo   Marc Gabriel   Anthony Golebiewski   Salvatore Gugliotta   Douglas Henderson
Paul Hobelmann   Cory Hunnicut   Annette Jeronczyk   Stephen Johnson   Orlando Karpf   J. Fred Kaulbach   Cheryl Keown   Lila Khalvati
Robert Khurana   Harvey Kirk   Hana Kolton-Patsouris   David LaCount   Leroy Landers   Danielle Lee   Kenneth Leibowitz   Xiaofeng Ma
Xiaoyi Ma   Robert Maloney   Amy Manley   Thomas Manning   Stuart Mardeusz   Tari Maynor   Lois McCue   Jonathan Moeller
Lennox Mohammed   Blair Monagle   Andrew Moore   Robert Morrison   Christina Neumann   Gregg Olmstead   Kevin Olsavsky
Jason Olsen   Kai Olsen   Anthony Pai   Raynold Paradis   Michael Petulla   Sarla Patel   Henry Pinto   Ellen Prantl-Bartlett   Bonnie Prentice
Timothy Quirk   Stephen Reimer   Christopher Rose   Michael Schwarz   Jeffrey Sears   Gene Smierciak   Claire Strugnell   Michael Swift
Donald Tangarone   Dana Tanimoto   Michael Tortora   Paul Tricome   Jenna Trotzer   Josie Tustin   Thomas Van Dean   Whitney Van Dean
Bruce Werfel   Richard Wilson   Cathy Wolfe   Scott Winger   Joe Ziegler   Zhen Zhang   Junfu Zhu   Elizabeth J. Zipf   **Architecture**
Lara Abisaleh   Bailey Allred   Karen Anderson   Mark Anderson   Joey Ayson   Christine Bacha-Rizk   Dean Belcher   Francois Benoit
Melissa Bernstein   Jonathan Betts   Adam Blood   Brian Boettger   Jason Boris   Gavin Bowie   Barbara Boylan O'Connell   Jeffrey Branter
Steffen Brinkmann   Paul Bui   Cesar Cacayan   David Canio   Edward Castro   Rico Cedro   Wen Hung Chen   Benjamin Collins
Emma Corbalan   Michael Crehan   Yang Dai   Rori Dajao   Scott Daniels   Virajita Dankar   Kelly Dapra Anderson   Paul D'Onofrio   Michael
Dorman   Laurent de Comarmond   Jeanna DeFazio Ventura   Paul Desjardins   Juliette Dolle   K. Darvin Dombach   Peter Dugo
Dan Edenbaum   David Esch   Pooneh Fassihi   Timothy Fells   Jonathan Fertig   Lloyd Fisk   Ryan Folger   Paul Francisco   William Fratick, Jr.
Donald Gallegos   Neil Garrioch   Tomasz Gawron-Gawrzynski   Ted Givens   Daniel Gobel   Katelyn Gosselin   Corey Graham   Sarah Greenawalt
Christina Guerrero   Jessica Hamilton   John Hammer   Andrea Hauber   Eric Heinsohn   Robert Hibbard   Davin Hong   Yong Il Hur
John Jackson   Edward Jenkins   Jeffrey E. Kahn   Bruce Keller   James Kelly-Rand   Paul Kleykamp   Michael Kolonauski   Thapawcc Kuhakarn
Leena Kurian   Neil Lahav   Ghazal Lajervardi   Jill Lavine   Chang Lee   Jong Hyeok Lee   Mun Seok Lee   Eric Levin   Shouning Li
James Libby   Frank Lucas   Qingyun Ma   Ali Mahjouri   Erin Mahoney   John Martell   Desmond McAuley   David McClintock   Charles McGloughlin
Allen McSparron   Pablo Meninato   Stephen Messinger   Anthony Miksitz   Walter Milano   David Miles   Tammy Miller   Eric Mitchell
Young Pil Moon   Donleroy Morales   May Narisaranukul   Brian Newswanger   Jason Niebish   Elizabeth Norwood   Francesca Oliveira

Judith Osers John Ostland Dana Ozik Heewon Park Julie Parker Eric Poon Chris Portner Kenneth Preaster Peter Rudd Francis Peltier Gerry Peria Serm Permsap Kriss Pettersen Gerry Power M. Sean Pulsifier Moshfequr Rahman Mark Reyer Mark Rhoades Rocco Rinaudo Bruce Ryan Grazyna Samborska Soha Shah Erin Sharp Naoko Shinozawa Keena Simon Paisarn Siricharoenwong John Sivills Michael Smith So-ok Son Michael Soucy Hal Spiers Robert Stasi David Steele Andrew Sternberg David Stomatuk Bernard Suber Lillian Sung Daniel Sweigart Max Swyder Yossapol Tangsuphoom Boris Torres Kevin Tracy Addis Valentine Ximena Valle Ariel Vazquez Sarah Vekasy Veronica Viggiano Sonal Vora Xu Wang Joseph Wynn Takeshi Yamada Hyeon Wug Yu Jing Yu Paolo Zavala Dennis Zhang Yihang Zheng Gregory Zielinski **Interiors** Alice Ardito Amritakar Bajwa Michelle Banfe Edward Barnett Joanne Barrera Craig Barbieri Lori Bertinelli Sue Best Christina Blumbach Richard Bolger Megan Broderick Brian Brooks Mimi Campbell Andrew Derrickson Pier Derrickson Royce Epstein Robin Fortenberry Maryn Gemgnani Judy Ginieczki Christopher Hanes Linda Hockenbury Gay Keller-Cattie Susan Kennedy Julian Looney Danielle Masucci Lisa McGregor Olga Mogilyansky Jennifer Nye Takashi Okuma Jacalyn Price Pollock Jessica Rubin Anthony Saby Allison Schadel Jennifer Sherman Sherri Smith Shane Strickler Dinesh Tharmaratnam Jennifer Thorsen Nisha Tiwari Lee Tomaccio Tina Tsaganos Ivar Viehe-Naess Cassandra Wagner Kerry Keith Wallace Christine Wirkkala Melissa Woods **MEP** Thomas Alessi Anson Alfano Richard Aliff Stephen Arey Walter Brown Jonathan Burke Lawrence Corbin Dennis Cruz Katherine Cunningham Phillip Cunningham Kha Dang Gary Debes Justin Delecki James Demers Michael Diamond Andrew DiSanti Gary DiSanti Mario DiTanno James Drew Gregory Farzetta, III Louis Fiorella Jeffrey Fisher William Flurer, Jr. Michael Futryk Charles Gibson Mugurel Giurgiu Robert Hackett Matthew Harper Ronald Height Eric Heinsohn Meghan Homa David Hunsberger Barry Hutchinson John Kampmeyer, Jr. Ashley Kenyon Kavi Khatri Allen Kozin Alexis Kreft Michael Kuha, Jr. Karl Labe John LaRosa Herbert Laskin Stephanie Mages Eugene Mamrol Steven Marafino Amanda Martz Edward McBride Amelia McCracken Benedetta Merceir Tracey Merritt Matthew Mitchell Eugene Mitman, III Anthony Nocito Wayne Petrella David Potchak Clinton Quarterman Anthony Reilly Warren Reuther Pat Rosati Richard Ryan, III Kevin Schaefer Rebecca Seitzmeyer William Short Paul Silva Gregory Smiley Hank Smith Wesley Smith, III Mary Strieffler Thomas Tran Soner Unver Steven Vesci **Site/Civil** Christopher Basse Mark Battaglia Anneliza Carmalt Michael Coyle Michael Domboski Terra Edenhart-pepe Donald Gallagher Thomas Grahame Jennifer Johnson Kestra Kelly Hugh McFadden Michael McKeever Jennifer Mui Maneesha Patel Marisa Razi Igor Rizanow Chris Rummler Kevin Selger John Templeton David Traczykiewicz **Structural** Florencia Acuna Kenneth Berlin David Brook Joydeep Chatterjee Ronald Connor Leo Doyer Gregory Eckel Larry Fahnstock Stephen Hess Janelle Meagher Henry Mercaldo Zachary Nord Kenneth O'Kelly-Lynch James Justin Purcell Fazlur Rahman Fabio Rosas Eli Rutkoski Heather Schreiber Robert Smith Christopher Swoyer Gabrielle Trout Anthony Viscusi Jesse Young Michael Zecca Shauna Zhang Xiaofeng Bill Zhang **Support/Administration** Michael DiGiacomo Howard Elgart Janka Fazekas John Harryman Jonathan Kravitz Thomas Lauletta Deanna Miller Alison Reilly Jesus Araujo Peter Blanchette Armando Correia Paul Eberle In Joong Eum Alexandra Goral William Gray Daniel Harrigan Timothy Heinze Wayne Mark Anthony Mendez Mary Micucci Edward Miller Mary Mills Marcus Lorenz Kiet Nguyen Robert Saulin Mark Svehlik Sherry Bailey Dionne Bannis Shannon Bass Roberta Bates Catherine Boyd Megan Benkert Marites Bradley Kelly Bramble Robert Bruno Lisa Burgos Joel Cardenas, Jr. Janet Carpenter Anna Carrara Felicia Chancy Jillian Cianfrini Katie Cipolla Frances Clements Amy Crotty Debra Daly Stephanie Daly William Daly Heather DiGiacomo Stephen D'intino Nicole Dorian Michaela Elliott Alice Eppolite Jonathan Fetherolf Teresa Gallagher Sabina Gallinari Michalina Goral James Granroth Susan Granroth Joseph Harrigan Rose Harrigan Mary Christine Jaje Lynn Markisz Charles Mayer Christine Matkowski Christina Mazurek Dianne McCurdy Patricia McGuire Aaron Miller Minzell Miree David Moyer Raquel Murray Gregory Oaster Catherine Olds Kevin Pearson George Peddle Johanne Pierre Eleanor Pluguez Kimberly Powell Cheryl Reyes Marquita Rose Marcin Rula Christine Sarin Luann Skwirut Nicole Spigner Sara Sproviero Anne Marie Stanton Jason Trojanowski Tracy Tzen Dina Williams Stu Willson Brigette Winbush

AWARDS & HONORS

Projects featured in this monograph:

2007

American Institute of Architects
Pennsylvania Society of Architects
Citation of Merit
Zhiye Plaza Office Tower
Suzhou, China

American Institute of Architects
Washington, DC Chapter
Merit Award for Excellence
FDA Central Shared Use Facility
Silver Spring, Maryland

International Interior Design Association
Philadelphia City Center Chapter
Best of Corporate Award
Brandywine Realty Trust Headquarters
Radnor, Pennsylvania

Business Week / Architectural Record
Award of Excellence
Novartis Institutes for Biomedical
Research New Global Research HQ
Cambridge, Massachusetts

2006

American Institute of Architects
North Carolina Chapter
Merit Award
BD Technologies Data Center
Raleigh, North Carolina

American Institute of Architects
Technology in Architectural Practice
Jury's Choice Award BIM
Merck Research Laboratories Boston
Boston, Massachusetts

International Interior Design Association
Philadelphia City Center
Best of Corporate Design
Elsevier Medical Publishing Office
Philadelphia, Pennsylvania

American Institute of Architects
Pennsylvania Society of Architects
Silver Medal
322 A Street, LLC
Wilmington, Delaware

American Institute of Architects
Pennsylvania Society of Architects
Citation of Merit
University of Colorado RC1
Auroroa, Colorado

Building Design & Construction
Gold Award
US Postal Service Processing and
Distribution Center
Philadelphia, Pennsylvania

2005

American Institute of Architects
Philadelphia Chapter
Gold Medal
322 A Street, LLC
Wilmington, Delaware

R&D Magazine
Renovated Laboratory of the Year
Novartis Institutes for Biomedical
Research New Global Research HQ
Cambridge, Massachusetts

American Institute of Architects
Philadelphia Chapter
Award of Recognition
University of Colorado RC1
Aurora, Colorado

American Institute of Architects
Boston Society of Architects
Award for Design
Merck Research Laboratories Boston
Boston, Massachusetts

American Institute of Architects
New England Chapter
Citation for Design Excellence
Merck Research Laboratories Boston
Boston, Massachusetts

American Institute of Architects
Pennsylvania Society of Architects
Merit Award for Design Excellence
Merck Research Laboratories Boston
Boston, Massachusetts

Department of Health and Human Services
FDA Commissioner's Special Citation
FDA Campus Consolidation
Silver Spring, Maryland

2004

American Institute of Architects
Philadelphia Chapter
Gold Medal
Merck Research Laboratories Boston
Boston, Massachusetts

American Institute of Architects
Philadelphia Chapter
Honor Award
Zhiye Plaza Office Tower
Suzhou, China

American Institute of Architects
Philadelphia Chapter
Award of Recognition
Wyeth Pharmaceutical Headquarters
Collegeville, Pennsylvania

American Institute of Architects
North Carolina Chapter
Merit Award for Design
FDA Life Sciences Laboratory
Silver Spring, Maryland

American Institute of Architects
Triangle NC Chapter
Honor Award
FDA Central Shared Use Facility
Silver Spring, Maryland

2003

American Institute of Architects
Philadelphia Chapter
Recognition Award
322 A Street, LLC
Wilmington, Delaware

2002

American Institute of Architects
Boston Society of Architects
Honor Award
United States Embassy
Singapore

American Institute of Architects
Philadelphia Chapter
Honor Award
University of Colorado RC1
Aurora, Colorado

2001

American Institute of Architects
Philadelphia Chapter
Honor Award
New England Bio Labs
Ipswich, Massachusetts

Urban Land Institute
Awards for Excellence Competition
Winner
Venetian Casino Resort
Las Vegas, Nevada

2000

American Institute of Architects
Philadelphia Chapter
Honor Award
Gov. of China Customs Complex
Shenzhen, China

American Institute of Architects
New Jersey Society of Architects
Silver Medal
Merck & Co., Inc., Multi-Science Facility
Rahway, New Jersey

American Institute of Architects
Pennsylvania Society of Architects
Award for Design Excellence
SAP America, Inc.
Newtown Square, Pennsylvania

American Institute of Architects
Philadelphia Chapter
People's Choice Award
University of Colorado HSC
Aurora, Colorado

Delaware County Planning Commission
William H. Bates Memorial Award
SAP America, Inc.
Newtown Square, Pennsylvania

1999

American Institute of Architects
Las Vegas Chapter
Honor Award
Delmonico Steakhouse
Las Vegas, Nevada

American Institute of Archtiects
Las Vegas Chapter
Merit Award
Venetian Casino Resort
Las Vegas, Nevada

American Institute of Architects
Philadelphia Chapter
Award for Design Excellence
SAP America, Inc.
Newtown, Pennsylvania

American Institute of Architects
New England Regional Design
Award Recipient
US Embassy
Singapore

Research and Development Magazine
Lab of the Year Award
Special Mention for Design Excellence
Aventis Pharmaceuticals, Inc.,
Bridgewater, New Jersey

1995

British Industry Awards
Supreme Award
Building of the Year Award
GlaxoSmithKline Headquarters
Stevenage, United Kingdom

1993

American Institute of Architects
Brick in Architecture Award
Drexel University
LeBow Engineering Building
Philadelphia, Pennsylvania

1992

American Society of Landscape Architects
Northern California Chapter
Merit Award
Ronald Reagan Presidential Library
Simi Valley, California

Building Stone Institute
Tucker Architectural Award
Bell Atlantic Properties
Bell Atlantic Tower
Philadelphia, Pennsylvania

1991

American Institute of Architects
Philadelphia Chapter
Merit Award
Drexel University Engineering
Philadelphia, Pennsylvania

International Marble Awards Program
Award
Bell Atlantic Properties
Bell Atlantic Tower
Philadelphia, Pennsylvania

American Institute of Architects
Pennsylvania Society of Architects
Distinguished Building Award
Drexel University Engineering
Philadelphia, Pennsylvania

1989

American Institute of Architects
New England Chapter
Honor Award
Treasury Buiilding
Singapore

American Institute of Architects
Boston Society of Architects
Boston Exports Award
Treasury Building
Singapore

1988

American Planning Association
National Planning Award
Carnegie Center
Princeton, New Jersey

1986

American Institute of Architects
Boston Society of Architects
Boston Exports Award
Pacwest Center
Portland, Oregon

1985

American Institute of Architects
Philadelphia Chapter
Gold Medal Award
Villanova University, Student Center
Villanova, Pennsylvania

American Institute of Architects
Portland Chapter
Honor Award
Pacwest Center
Portland, Oregon

1982

Harleston Parker Gold Medal
Federal Reserve Bank of Boston
Boston, Massachusetts

1981

R.S. Reynolds Memorial Award for
Distinguished Architecture Using
Aluminum
Citicorp Center
New York, New York

1979

American Intitute of Architects
National Honor Award
Citicorp Center
New York, New York

American Institute of Architects
The New England Regional Council
Award for Excellence in Architecture
Federal Reserve Bank of Boston
Boston, Massachusetts

American Institute of Architects
Philadelphia Chapter
Silver Medal Design of Excellence
Community College of Philadelphia
Philadelphia, Pennsylvania

1978

American Institute of Architects
Boston Society of Architects
Award for Excellence
Citicorp Center
New York, New York

American Institute of Architects
New York State Association of Architects
Certificate of Merit
Citicorp Center
New York, New York

American Institute of Architects
New York Chapter
Outstanding Contribution
Citicorp Center
New York, New York

1975

American School & University
Architectural Competition
Top Honors
University of Connecticut Health Center
Farmington, Connecticut

1974

American Institute of Architects
Pennsylvania Society of Architects
First Honor Award
University of Connecticut Health Center
Farmington, Connecticut

American Institute of Architects
Pennsylvania Society of Architects
First Honor Award
International Monetary Fund
Washington, DC

1969

American Institute of Architects
Philadelphia Chapter
Gold Medal Award
Cafeteria, The Monsanto Company
St. Louis, Missouri

American Institute of Architects
National Honor Award
Cafeteria, The Monsanto Company
St. Louis, Missouri

1967

American Institute of Architects
Architectural Firm Award
Hugh Stubbins and Associates

American Institute of Architects
Philadelphia Chapter
Citation for Excellence
Concordia Lutheran College
Ann Arbor, Michigan

American Institute of Architects
National Honor Award
Municipal Services Building
Philadelphia, Pennsylvania

1966

American Institute of Architects
National Award of Merit
Swarthmore College Dining Hall
Swarthmore, Pennsylvania

1965

American Institute of Architects
Philadelphia Chapter
Gold Medal
Municipal Services Building
Philadelphia, Pennsylvania

American Institute of Architects
Philadelphia Chapter
Silver Medal
Swarthmore College Dining Hall
Swarthmore, Pennsylvania

1964

American Institute of Architects
New Jersey Society of Architects
Award of Merit
Concordia Lutheran College
Ann Arbor, Michigan

American Institute of Architects
Pennsylvania Society of Architects
Honor Award
Concordia Lutheran College
Ann Arbor. Michigan

American Institute of Architects
National Honor Award
Molecular Electronic Laboratory
Westinghouse Corp.
Baltimore, Maryland

1963

American Institute of Architects
New Jersey Society of Architects
Commendation of Preliminary Design
Municipal Services Building
Philadelphia, Pennsylvania

1962

Progressive Architecture
Design Awards Program
First Design Award
Municipal Services Building
Philadelphia, Pennsylvania

American Intitute of Architects
Philadelphia Chapter
Gold Medal
American Cyanamid Company
Corporate Headquarters
Wayne, New Jersey

American Institute of Architects
Pennsylvania Society of Architects
Honor Award
American Cyanamid Company
Corporate Headquarters
Wayne, New Jersey

1960

American Institute of Architects
New Jersey Society of Architects
Award of Merit
National Headquarters,
The Monsanto Company
St. Louis, Missouri

1958

Brussels Universal and International
Worlds Fair Exhibit
The Lankenau Hospital
Overbrook, Pennsylvania

1954

American Institute of Archtiects
New Jersey Society of Architects
Award of Merit
The Lankenau Hospital
Overbrook, Pennsylvania

American Institute of Architects
National Honor Award
The Lankenau Hospital
Overbrook, Pennsylvania

1953

American Institute of Architects
New Jersey Society of Architects
Award of Merit
Phoenixville Hospital
Phoenixville, Pennsylvania

American Institute of Architects
Philadelphia Chapter
Gold Medal
Phoenixville Hospital
Phoenixville, Pennsylvania

1950

American Institute of Architects
New Jersey Society of Architects
Award of Merit
The Lankenau Hospital
Overbrook, Pennsylvania

American Institute of Architects
Philadelphia Chapter
Special Commendation
The Lankenau Hospital
Overbrook, Pennsylvania

1949

American Institute of Architects
Philadelphia Chapter
Gold Medal
A.J. Peaslee Beach House
Mantoloking, New Jersey

PHOTOGRAPHY CREDITS

Peaslee Beach House
Photographer: Robert Damora

Lankenau Hospital
Photographer: Lawrence S. Williams

Sharpe House
Photographer: Joseph Molitor

Berlin Congress Hall
Photographer: Nick Merrick/Hedrich Blessing

Municipal Services Building
Photographer: Balthazar Korab

University of Connecticut Health Center
Photographer: Tom Crane/Tom Crane Photography Inc.

Citicorp Center
Photographer: Nick Merrick/Hedrich Blessing, Edward Jacoby/
Jacoby Photography, Norman McGrath/Norman McGrath
Photographer Inc.

Federal Reserve Bank of Boston
Photographer: Edward Jacoby/Jacoby Photography, Peter
Vanderwarker/PV Photos, Nick Wheeler © Frances Loeb Library,
Harvard Design School

Drexel University Engineering Center
Photographer: C. Geoffrey Berken

Ronald Reagan Presidential Library
Photographer: Edward Jacoby/Jacoby Photography

Bell Atlantic Tower
Photographer: Timothy Hursley

Landmark Tower – Minato Mirai 21
Photographs Courtesy of Mitsubishi Estate Co. and Courtesy of
Nikko Hotels

GlaxoSmithKline Medicines Research Centre
Photographer: Dennis Gilbert

US Embassy Ambassador's Residence / Chancery Building
Photographer: (Residence) Timothy Griffith/Esto Photographics
Inc., (Chancery Building) Hans Schlupp

US FDA Headquarters Consolidation – Master Plan
Photographers: Ron Solomon/Ron Solomon Photography and
Alain Jaramillo

Dow Jones & Company Bernard Kilgore Center
Photographer: Jeff Goldberg/Esto Photographics Inc.

SAP North American Headquarters
Photographer: Jeff Goldberg/Esto Photographics Inc.

Venetian Resort Hotel Casino
Photographers: Glenn Cormier/InSite Architectural Photography,
Peter Malinowski/InSite Architectural Photography, Erhard Pfeiffer/
Erhard Pfoiffer Photographer

Delmonico Steakhouse
Photographer: Paul Bardagjy/Paul Bardagjy Photography

Datek World Headquarters
Photographer: Tom Crane/Tom Crane Photography Inc.

Wyeth Pharmaceutical Headquarters
Photographer: Paul Warchol Photography

Johnson & Johnson Drug Discovery Laboratory
Photographer: Tom Bonner/Tom Bonner Photography

NBC Today Show Olympic Pavilion
Photographer: Woodruff/Brown Architectural Photography

MITRE Center
Photographer: Peter Vanderwarker/PV Photos

Novartis World Headquarters
Photographer: Jeff Goldberg/Esto Photographics Inc.

**University of Colorado Health Sciences Center, Research
Complex 1**
Photographer: Ron Johnson/Ron Johnson Photography

Merck Research Laboratories Boston
Photographer: Paul Warchol Photography and Christopher Barnes
Photography

322 "A" Street Office and Manufacturing Building
Photographer: Woodruff/Brown Architectural Photography

BD Technologies Data Center and Office Expansion
Photographer: James West/JWest Productions

USPS Processing and Distribution Center
Photographer: Woodruff/Brown Architectural Photography

Elsevier Health Sciences Headquarters
Photographer: Tom Crane/Tom Crane Photography Inc.

Digitas World Headquarters
Photographer: Robert Benson/Robert Benson Photography

Zhiye Plaza Office Tower
Photographer: Shen Zhonghai

University of Colorado Health Sciences Center, Research Complex 2
Photographer: Ron Johnson/Ron Johnson Photography

US FDA Headquarters Consolidation—Central Shared Use
Photographer: Ron Solomon/Ron Solomon Photography and Alain Jaramillo

St. Lawrence University
Photographer: Woodruff/Brown Architectural Photography

Brandywine Realty Trust Corporate Headquarters
Photographer: Tom Crane/Tom Crane Photography Inc.

ACKNOWLEDGMENTS

We would like to express our sincere gratitude to those whose efforts and contributions were important to the creation of this book. To our clients, for providing opportunities for creativity, expression, and the possibility of distinction, and for allowing us to be involved in realizing their aspirations. And to our design staff, whose uncompromising determination, ardent dedication, sleepless nights, and occasional blind faith were responsible for the achievements evidenced in the preceding pages.

We would also like to specifically acknowledge Jason Trojanowski for his art direction and layouts, Cathy Boyd for handling the image representation, Tracy Tzen for compiling and proofreading the text, and Leonardo Diaz, Liz Zipf, and Katie Cipolla for their overall support.

INDEX